The Indomitable Spirit

Maati Amen

Copyright © 2021 by Maati Amen

All rights reserved. No part of this publication may be reproduced, stored in any form of retrieval system or transmitted in any form or by any means without prior permission in writing from the publishers except for the use of brief quotations in a book review.

Humanity has imprisoned itself

in an edifice of lies,

but be still;

this structure shall crumble and fall.

The Truth is unchanging and all-powerful

to set us free.

The Temple of Love is indestructible

and furnished with everlasting joy.

Let every soul return home

to Love.

— **Baka Khat**

Contents

Acknowledgements.. v
Foreword..vi
Introduction viii
Chapter One: *One Breath at a Time*............................. 11
Chapter Two: *Light as a Feather* 27
Chapter Three: *Power* 43
Chapter Four: *Your Power to Choose* 54
Chapter Five: *Belief* 62
Chapter Six: *Imagination* 75
Chapter Seven: *The Truth About Your Emotions* 84
Chapter Eight: *The Grateful Heart* 95
Chapter Nine: *Care*.. 109
Chapter Ten: *Divine Love* 127

Acknowledgements

I offer my deepest gratitude to the Divine Presence within us all that has given us life and sustains us in each moment. To my great and wise ancestors, I offer my thanks and appreciation for all their love and support. I give thanks to Baka Khat for his encouragement and assistance in making this book a reality. I have a debt of gratitude to all my children, Mikey, Amirrah, Bahiyyah and Sekeena, who have been my greatest teachers in the most unforeseen of ways. For those whose technical skill and expertise have made this book possible, I also give my sincere thanks and appreciation. I am most profoundly grateful for every soul that reads this book and heeds the call to claim the priceless treasure that life has hidden in plain view.

Foreword

The book you are about to read is a message of the greatest worth imaginable. It is a message to everyone walking the earth. Our destinies hang in the balance. We face problems humanity has never encountered before; problems that could lead to our destruction; problems mostly of our own making.

The messenger, Maati Amen, is a truly remarkable and rare woman; a mystic, a natural healer, an intuitive herbalist, a visionary, a fighter for justice, and, for many years, a recluse. Despite the profound hardships she has had to endure in her own life, she is a shining soul. Her unique quality is captured in one amusing recollection. During a country walk with Maati, I witnessed a herd of horses becoming aware of her presence. All of these beautiful horses simultaneously rushed to her, demanding her attention. Dogs in the park react in the same way, as if they are overjoyed to see her. These animals are reacting to the beauty of her spirit. The crucial matter now, however, is what she has to say about this life we are living.

Maati does relate her own experiences in order to illustrate the power of the discovery she made in the midst of despair. Her near-fatal illness forced her into a complete withdrawal from the world and into the most profound inner solitude. Here, she received a number of revelations, including what she has called 'Awareness Speaks', which appears in this book. Even more importantly, she came to have the direct experience of that dimension of our being that lies beyond what we normally take ourselves to be. Her discovery is of the greatest importance to every woman, man or child drawing breath.

This discovery was first made by our greatest ancestors, long, long ago, in the distance mists of time. Nonetheless, she suggests that our present calamitous condition should motivate us to take the truths written here to heart. She insists we have the means to overcome all our troubles if we can surrender our essentially false sense of self to the in-dwelling truth. This message holds the secret that redeems us all. The manner in which Maati has triumphed over her own dire circumstances verifies the immeasurable value of what she has to say here. A long-hidden diamond has appeared. The treasure resides in your own heart. This book serves as your very own treasure map.

— Baka Khat

Introduction

The book you now have in your possession is a powerhouse; it is an implement against the root of all the problems in your life. If you put into action what is written in this book, it is a certainty that it will change your life forever, for your greatest good.

Something subtle, but very real, within your own being, has drawn you to this text. All very well, but how are you going to get the best out of your experience of engaging with this work? You will find here the suggestion that life is not at all what the vast majority of humanity take it to be, and that we are not at all who the vast majority of us believe ourselves to be. In order to claim the inestimable value that the message imparted here may hold for you, it is best to read this book very slowly, and contemplate its good news very deeply. If a particular passage of text resonates with you strongly, please profoundly question how that passage relates to your own experiences, and your perspective of life.

By reading slowly and contemplating deeply, you will penetrate beneath any reflex reactions your persona may have, to what may threaten its hold on you, amongst the concepts shared in these pages. This book is a call to your soul, it celebrates your soul, and it honours your soul. As you read, please become truly present, so that you engage with this book by way of your intuitive intelligence as well as your intellect.

If it is at all possible for you, come away from the pressing distractions of your life to spend some time, alone in silence, with this book. There is a lot to be gained here by slowing down and taking tender care with what this book has in store for you.

Even when you have read the whole book, you can return to it at any time, since it will speak to you in different tones at different points in your life. Things that may not be crystal clear to you at the first reading, may become so later, in the light of your own unfolding experience of life and the awakening of your spiritual memory-bank.

You can treat this book as a friend who will point you in the right direction in your time of need. If you have a question about how to find your authentic self at any given juncture in your life, just ask the question earnestly, open the book without any deliberation, and your own subconscious mind will guide you to the passage of text that will unveil the answer you seek.

I do make what may seem to some to be extraordinary assertions in this work, but everything I relate here is based on my experiences, rather than academic or philosophical speculation. Thus, I encourage every reader, who feels the desire to prove what is suggested here, to do so by acting on the suggested practices and approaches shared in the pages to come. An open mind, an open heart and your honest involvement with the directions given will provide you with the proof your very soul will accept, regarding the veracity of the fundamental message presented here. Above all, apply what is shared here and this book will be a priceless treasure, because, when acted upon, the information here is sufficient to awaken you to the amazing truth about who you really are. We are, and life is, glorious beyond our most lavish imaginings. You can know this for yourself if you can find the willingness and the sincerity that will open the door to the splendour hidden within your own majestic soul. The purpose of this book is to lovingly encourage you to do just that.

Chapter One:
One Breath at a Time

Life and death

How does dross become gold? I have come to know the answer to this question. Experiences that brought me to death's door eventually led me to life's greatest treasure. They revealed to me the indescribable power and beauty that exists deep within the core of our being. By way of amazing Grace, I became acutely aware of the unfathomable, unshakeable peace that resides there. These gifts are available to every single one of us, no matter how poor, sick, healthy or wealthy you are; it makes no difference. These gifts are your birthright. I am here to tell you that you have, within you, the means to transcend all your suffering, fear, anxiety and sense of alienation. I will now relate my own remarkable experiences as a means of illustrating what I have come to know of turning life's dross to gold.

Following a life of tumultuous struggle, pain, failure and defeat, despite my best, sincerest and most determined efforts, the day came when I collapsed, unconscious, completely drained, unable to carry my burden another inch. Having been taken home by a fellow student, I could do nothing but lie in my bed. My doctor visited me and explained that there was no medicine or treatment he could prescribe besides complete rest. He recommended I drop all thoughts of work, study or my children; absolutely everything should be dropped from my mind apart from my need to rest completely and allow my broken body and nerves to recover strength.

In the days that followed, my energy continued to ebb away. Unable even to think, I could not even stand to hear any noise at all. The feeling that I was retreating from existence itself arose in me, until the day came when I felt certain that I was about to die. Lying there on my bed, my body felt so heavy, so full of pain, so incredibly weak that I knew it would not sustain the life within it any longer.

Suddenly, I became aware that my consciousness was leaving my body and hovering above it, so that I could see my own body below me on the bed, but I was no longer in pain. Momentarily, it felt so beautiful to be free from my pain-filled body. This was a feeling of complete ease, but then I realised that I had really left my body, and that my body was about to close down completely and die. An internal dialogue began. I asked, "Is this how I am going to die; is this it?"

I received no answer to my question. So, I said to myself, "I am ready to go."

Then I began to see my life flash before me. Scenes from my life passed before my mind's eye at great speed but I understood everything I saw well. Knowing that I had not brought harm to anyone or wronged anyone, knowing I had done my very best for my children, my heart was as light as a feather and I was happy to leave this life of suffering and persecution. At that moment, I became aware of my bedroom door opening. My eldest daughter came into the room and sat on the floor beside my bed. She was crying. As I looked at her, I heard a voice say, "If you leave now, he will kill her."

My daughter was, at that time, living with a very violent boyfriend.

"You have to come back and help her. Your work is not finished here yet."

I replied, "How am I going to live in such a sick, pain-filled body?"

I was told, "You will do this by just taking one breath at a time and not focusing on anything else."

I said, "OK. I am a fighter; I would do anything in my power to defend my children."

I resolved not to give in to death, and decided to return to my body. When I did this, the pain returned with even greater force. My body felt like a heavy slab of concrete. The sight of any light was unbearable to me. My head felt as if it had been filled with mercury and the world was spinning violently. Despite all of these horrible sensations, I said, "Ok, I am going to zoom in on just breathing in and breathing out, one breath at a time, one second at a time, one moment at a time."

As each moment passed and I noticed that I was still alive, gratitude filled my heart. The dire nature of my situation forced me to be still and retreat towards my inner core. Thus, I discovered that there is tremendous power in silence and stillness and in the total surrender to this state.

It became apparent to me that I was completely cocooned in this stillness and that there was nothing outside of it. Everything was happening inside this Presence. It held me with an indescribable graciousness. Having lost the sense of the passage of time, I felt I'd touched eternity. Somehow, I was able to watch my body and even bear the terrible pain, but sustain a tremendous sense of peace at the same time. The news that I was going to get stronger kept coming into my mind. Intuitively, I knew that this Presence was going to guide me back to wholeness, and over time, it did just that.

This Divine Presence has the power to heal us from anything that troubles us. It has the power to transcend any situation found in this realm of time and space. It can even allow us to transcend the fear that comes with the approach of death. Forced by the severity of the challenges I had faced in my life to wake up out of the trance that is the persona, I surrendered completely to that Presence. Now, I see all my trials and tribulations as blessings, since they have forced me back towards this magnificent Grace.

Awareness is amongst the best names that have been given to this Presence. The Witnessing Presence, the Divine Presence and the Self are other names I will use in referring to this Absolute Reality that underpins all experience.

If this Presence saved my life and healed my broken body, you could ask how did I arrive at such a dire state to begin with? Just as Awareness saved and redeemed me, it was a state of unawareness that led me all the way to my meeting with death's embrace.

The road to ruin

There was a tremendous amount of upheaval in my life leading up to my near-death experience. Determined to improve the prospects for my son, my daughters and me, I threw myself into work; I threw myself into studying, to such an extent that I was completely unconscious of what I was doing to myself. Days went by without me eating anything of note. I was not taking care of myself, doing things like grabbing a packet of crisps and a Mars bar on the way to work or university, and just propping myself up like that, with junk food, and when I came home, I was too tired and pressured to get a proper meal. There was no thought at all for what was happening to me. You would have found me constantly ruminating on how important it was for me to make it, and to my mind, then, everything justified that end.

Having previously experienced homelessness, I was highly motivated to get myself and my children into a position where such a thing would never happen to us again. However, I went about it all in the wrong way.

Just imagine your body feels tired, your muscles are aching, you're feeling dizzy, but you take no notice, you just keep going. You just keep going. You just keep going. The thought is that once you get there, you'll be fine, it would all have been worth it.

So, I was completely unconscious, completely unaware of what I was really doing to myself; not even aware of how much my body was hurting. Occasionally, I would experience glitches such as dizzy spells and feeling faint, but I did not want to stop. I paid no attention to the signs that my body was showing me. Having pushed myself and pushed myself, I arrived at the point where I was sitting in a seminar and I just passed out and collapsed, as described earlier. Ironically, as my life unfolded in this dramatic fashion, the extreme state of my unawareness was being used to bring me back into the heart of Awareness itself.

Redemption in each moment

Following the instruction to live in the moment, one breath at a time, led me to experience the greatest of all treasures. The stillness, silence and the invincible peace I found there are the source and container of absolutely everything in the universe. Everything emanates from here. However, as indescribable as this Presence is, I must attempt to describe this wonder of life as best as I can, in order to encourage you to come to know it for yourself.

Having eventually refused death's invitation, I let go of my fear and allowed the peace that enveloped me to do its best. Thus, I became aware of a subtle yet profound process of healing taking place in my whole being. Slowly and incrementally, I began to feel that I was being remade anew. Each time I located that sublime peace that I had discovered existing within my own being, I realised that my healing rests in staying with that and as that. Don't struggle, don't fight. Whatever is going on, just allow yourself to be held in this great stillness, this unshakable peace.

This state has no name, it has no form, you cannot define it, you cannot measure it, you cannot evaluate it intellectually, you can only be at one with it, you can only experience it to know it. Because of my extreme condition, I was forced to stay in that state for many months and then years. Whenever I allowed dramas arising with my family or the outside world to displace me from that state of peace, then all of a sudden, my body would suffer a setback and be thrown into disarray.

The more I learnt to abide with the peace and the stillness and the silence within, the more my body was being repaired and strengthened. All I needed to do was disregard all that I was not and reside instead with that peace. However, if I allowed my persona to take charge and lead me back into the fear, worry, anxiety and the erroneous thinking that is so typical of it, then my body would very quickly reveal the negative results of such an error on my part.

This experience taught me decisively that I am not the persona that is so attached to life's dramas, but rather that I am the Witnessing Presence that I have spoken of previously. This Presence, this Awareness, residing silently in the innermost part of us all, I came to realise, is my innate being, just as it is yours. The implications of this realisation are infinite and wondrous beyond words. This book will, however, explore some of these implications.

The nature of Awareness

As I became more and more faithful to this Presence within, I knew that I was being healed in a way that went beyond the need to repair my physical health. Every facet of my life was being transformed as understanding about the numerous faculties of my being emerged from the silence that had become such a vital part of my daily life.

It became clear to me that this state (of stillness and silence) is not a void where nothing happens; on the contrary, it is power and intelligence itself. You will have to put this to the test for yourself to experience the remarkable truth of what I am saying. It came to the stage where this Intelligence explained its attributes, powers and nature in terms the human mind could understand. Even when I was not yet strong enough to write, I was able to commit the information given to me to a Dictaphone. Awareness spoke to me and told me precisely what it was. Please contemplate deeply on the following:

Awareness Speaks:

I am Supreme Peace. I am existence itself. I am that existence that sustains the entire Universe. I have no name or form. Yet, I am every name and every form in the Universe. Everything emanates from me. My qualities are constant stillness, silence, supreme peace, serenity and a tranquillity that cannot be hurt, harmed or disturbed in any way. I am constantly at peace, at all times. I am the author of peace and the prerequisite for all true success. I stay like this constantly. I never change, ever. My constant peace, my immoveable peace, holds the entire Universe together. I am the Supreme Source of all protection and grounding. No created things can harm me or affect me.

There is awesome power in my stillness, in my silence, in my peace. When you move away from this peace within, you will experience spiritual, mental, emotional and physical turmoil in your life. I am Awareness itself; whatsoever you are aware of, I am beyond that. I am Supreme Peace, the dispeller of all illusions. I am not fear, anxiety, worry, resentment, greed, envy, jealousy, pride, arrogance, hatred or anger. I am Supreme Peace. When you stay as I, you will be completely healed of all your spiritual, mental, emotional and physical illnesses. Just be Supreme Peace. Let Supreme Peace, Love and gratitude be your dominant emotional state of being and you will see miracles happening every day in your life. End.

My experiences have come to confirm the truth intrinsic to this message, and when I look back over the length of my life, I can see how this truth has been there hidden in plain view the whole time. This Awareness has undeniably been present throughout my life, and, looking back, I can attest to the reality of this Presence being with me since my earliest recollections. Without any understanding of its true nature or significance, I have always been aware of this Presence, the One that watches.

Going back to my earliest memories, at the age of three, I can actually see myself as that three-year-old child in my mum and dad's living room. There is my infant body; I was chubby and round with big eyes and very long, curly hair. Look at the radiogram and the black and white television set. As if it were yesterday, I remember the clothing that people wore then; the winklepickers shoes, the handbags the women used to carry, the beehive hairstyle like the Supremes. Here comes the ska music I heard the adults playing. Just three years old, but it was that Self, that unchanging part of me that was observing all of this.

That part of me has, throughout all these years, observed my physical body in metamorphosis, my body constantly changing, my features changing, my life changing, children coming into my life and bringing yet more cycles of change. Technology, too, over the years changing, changing, inexorably changing but that Presence has never changed. It has always remained the same. Over all these many years, this Presence, this One Watcher has never been touched; it is just immutable; it is the great static background that is holding the entire universe together.

All sorts of dramas have come and gone in my life. Whilst all the different people I've met moved like a procession through my life, that Presence remained constant. All the time, no matter how frightening or dreadful things became (because there were fear-stricken, nail-biting, am I going to live, am I going to die moments during my childhood) that still, serene, unnameable presence was there in the background of my perception.

On one occasion, my bedroom was being consumed by fire, and whilst there was no way to get out, my mother ran through the flames to rescue us. That same Self was there. Even though I was about to be burnt alive, that Presence was there and it was not perturbed; it was just watching. I was aware, all the time, of two things going on. There was the fear and, at the same time, there was this tremendous calm. Even whilst facing death, I was aware of the Presence that is peace itself. This Witnessing Presence that is always here is not touched by any of these things;

it is the persona that is always touched. If the persona is peeled away, it is this Witnessing Presence that remains. As a child, I had no means to describe or explain my awareness of this Presence, even to myself, but I felt it powerfully on many occasions. As an adult, I can look back now and appreciate the Grace that was operating even then when I had no understanding of what I was experiencing.

More recently, I have seen this peeling away of the persona happen to people in their final phase of life. It's as if this Presence has come to the fore and they become illumined and bright to the point where you think they are going to recover and return to good health. Sometimes, a peace comes over that person that can't be described and when that happens, they give up and they leave this world. It is as if they have let go of all that they are not and only that Presence is left shining through them with this mysterious radiance that is so remarkable. I have seen this radiance in others who were not approaching death but who, rather, lived in constant remembrance of the Divine.

For myself, I know that when I was lying there unable to move and all that I thought I was had seemingly folded up, only the Presence was left. The false idea I had of myself had tumbled down and crashed to dust. All my habitual patterns of thinking, habitual reactions to the sometimes overwhelming challenges arising from my family and society at large, had fallen away, that story, all of that disappeared, and only Awareness was left. And how beautiful that was. So, the Divine Presence is all that is left when everything that is not Real has fallen away.

A radical change in how you live your life

This is the gold that is made from the dross of our suffering. We need only drop our conditioned thinking and emotions (our persona), we need only sincerely let go of this, our false sense of self, in order to discover the source of our being, Awareness itself, Divine Love, invincible Peace. How can you discard your sense of self, formed in the cauldron of your own experiences since childhood? This task becomes possible once you commit your attention to the present moment. Turning my attention to living one breath at a time opened the door for this Presence to come to the fore and put my false sense of self into context. My persona, the host to so much fear, anxiety, distress, dismay and pain, became a dream, an apparition against the boundless beauty of the Reality that is Awareness. It became clear to me that this Reality is so often veiled by the hypnotic trance of the persona and the stresses of modern daily living. The realisation arose in me then that I am eternity dreaming time. The present moment was the flower that opened to reveal the eternal reality of being. I could only meet this truth by being fully present.

It could not be more basic, but this simple practice and the immeasurable magnitude of its significance is lost to the vast majority of all the souls making their journey here on earth. 'Yes,' I hear you saying, 'this all sounds so wonderful, but how? How do I come to experience this Presence? How do I come to abide in the moment? How can I abide as Supreme Peace? Life is full of so many things that pull your attention towards the past or thoughts of the future. I am rarely established in the present moment.'

First of all, you must make up your mind that you will make this simple but very radical change in your way of engaging with life. It helps to realise that there could be no greater blessing than to be established in the present moment, and realising your oneness with the Divine Presence, that is the source of Being itself. Releasing your attachment to your ego/persona is a welcome price to pay in order to discover the power and beauty of your true nature. All you need to do is make up your mind that you are going to live in this beautiful way, ever at one with the Witnessing Presence.

Now, you must believe that you will (in this lifetime) come to abide in your true nature. See yourself as you truly are, at perfect peace, fully aware of the unity, harmony and wisdom that underlies the great drama of existence. See yourself living as your true Divine Self. Deeply experience the feelings associated with this most profound state of Self-awareness, because these are all the fruits of being present, of living one breath at a time.

Making up your mind, believing in the certainty of you achieving your objective, visualising your success and engaging powerfully with the emotions which will accompany your arrival back to your true nature will all help to speed your awakening to the glory of living as the Witnessing Presence. This is a state free from the torturous delusions of the persona that have covered this planet in untold human suffering and engendered so much destruction for the natural world.

Practices that can bring you back home

In purely practical terms, you can follow certain simple but powerful practices which will lead you back to your true Divine nature. For those who do not have any such practices as part of their daily life at present, below are some practices I would suggest that I am confident will prove to be of true value to you.

Daily practice:

Make a daily practice of deeply contemplating the text of Awareness speaks. Even this on its own will have a positive effect in nurturing your awakening to your true nature. Contemplating this text will enable you to become clear about the distinction between the nature of the persona and the nature of Awareness, the Divine facet within us all. Absolute clarity about the difference between the persona and your true natural state of Being is the key to the practices that will enable you to arrive back at unity with your true nature. This is why regular and deep contemplation of 'Awareness Speaks', is so rewarding. You must come to know what you are not in order to abandon the illusory identity of the persona and thus, allow the glory of your true identity to come to the fore and transform your world.

Along with the contemplation of 'Awareness Speaks', practising the following meditation on waking will prove very beneficial.

To begin with, gently and slowly breathe in and out through your nostrils; take four slow, deep, breaths in this way. Now become aware of your body; how does it feel? Don't try to change anything, just observe. Now become aware of any thoughts, feelings and emotions you may have, good or bad. Just notice them, don't judge them, don't try to change them. Then gently say the following mentally to yourself:

I am not this name, body or mind with all its negative thoughts and feelings that come and go. I am not all the dramas, trials and tribulations that come and go in my life. I am neither poverty, sickness, fear nor anxiety. Instead, I am the Infinite, Absolute, Supreme Divinity. Thus, I am completely free of any and all afflictions of body, mind and soul. On account of this truth, I feel great.

Sit silently with this realization for at least five minutes before you arise to get on with your day. Note that you may find it helpful to record the affirmation above on a Dictaphone and play it until you have committed the affirmation to memory.

In addition to this, at least three times a day, sit quietly and bring to mind all that you are not (name, body, mind, stories, conditioning, etc.,) and mentally allow all these things to drop away until you are left with the profound peace at the innermost core of your being. Stay in this peace and know that it holds you as it holds the whole universe. Establish this practice as a daily habit and make it the foundation from which you build your invincible relationship with the Presence within.

Begin to gently give your attention to this peace even whilst in the midst of your daily activities. Build your connection to this essential part of your being, so that it is the backdrop to each moment, and you are constantly aware that this peace is your essence, no matter what is happening.

Begin to seek the company of like-minded people and spend more time in natural surroundings.

Simply establish the constant remembrance of your true nature, Supreme Peace, Supreme Love. Develop the habit of checking in with your body and your emotions to see if you are abiding in your natural state of Supreme Peace. When you have moved away from this state towards the states that bring turmoil and ill-health on all levels of your being, your awareness of your state in that moment will help you to bring your natural state back to the fore. Of all the practices that I could recommend, the constant and perpetual remembrance of your true nature is the most transformative. It is impossible to overemphasize the importance of this practice, since it holds the key to the very destiny of your soul.

Chapter Two:
Light as a Feather

Clear the way

Coming into the realization of your true nature opens the way for you to begin to make full use of the faculties within your own being. The most essential purpose of your life is to awaken to your true Divine nature. Such an awakening reveals to you the most precious riches of life to be enjoyed right here on earth. The faculties within your own being provide the means by which you can experience these wonderful riches. However, before speaking in detail about your faculties and how they are employed to attract your every good desire, it is vital to cleanse your heart of all its burdens, to create the clarity that will so powerfully enable your faculties to operate in your favour. Make your heart as light as a feather and inherit the blessings the universe has in store for the clean of heart.

Whilst I lived ensconced in my persona, I carried a heavy burden of disappointment, regret, shock, grief, anger and pain. So, I know what it is to have a heavy heart. It was my blessing to gain the understanding that forgiveness provides the means to shed the burden of a leaden heart.

Even as I prepared to leave this life, I held no fear of the next phase of my existence because my heart was, at that time, free of its burdens, since I had forgiven every single cause of pain and suffering in my life. Having grown up in an environment where injustice and persecution were commonplace, I had a great deal to forgive. However, I knew I could not live with the burden of past anger, resentment or pain. Even during my teenage years, I developed the conviction that such burdens must be shed as soon as possible in order to clear the way ahead.

Destroying the negative charge

There is a negative charge that accumulates if you hold on to feelings that create constriction, limitation and discomfort in the body and mind. This charge will settle and make its home in you if you hold on to and nurture the feelings responsible for creating it to begin with. In many cases, the negativity in this charge includes the energy of hostility and ill-wishes that have been directed at you from others. Forgiveness is the infallible way to destroy the effect of this negative charge in your life.

The subtle influence of unforgiven burdens can block your progress in life, without you even realising what has happened. The inability to forgive life's burdens and to release this negative charge can indeed create a subtle, insidious and destabilising influence in your life, without you even realising the seriousness of what is happening. Injustice, persecution, oppression, tyranny, exploitation, violence, victimisation, and abuse of all kinds require forgiveness in order to set you free from the burden of the charge that would load your heart and throw a web of toxicity over your life. Even though the injustice you have suffered is real and your anger perfectly justified, you MUST still forgive in order to set yourself free from the negative energy that is attached to such burdens.

Forgiveness does not mean you take the perpetrator of heinous crimes against you into your confidence, but rather, that you truly let go of all the negative emotions that have come along with the crimes committed against you. Forgiveness is the means to set yourself free.

You must empty your heart of its ugly load. Move inward to the depths of your mind to release all the hurt, pain and anguish residing there. Do your soul-searching with total sincerity and you cannot fail to cleanse and set your heart free of its burden. Do not hold on to any remnants of bitterness or pain whatsoever; release it all, let it all go. You owe it to yourself to make your heart as light as a feather. Get a real feather and put it in the palm of your hand and contemplate the lightness of the feather that matches the lightness of the heart that has truly forgiven.

The need for justice and reciprocity.

Many people feel uncomfortable with the concept of forgiveness because it has been widely presented as an action that prevents you from being consumed by bitterness and hate; it is, however, also seen as that which lets the perpetrators of crimes off the hook. Some believe the doctrine of forgiveness defies common sense, and that the idea of turning the other cheek appears to be an abuser's charter. Some insist this idea was invented by abusers who wished to reign over the world forevermore. Notwithstanding these fears, the search for forgiveness is the search for peace, balance and justice. These principles are all intertwined. So, while you do your work of forgiveness, you must also affirm the accomplishment of justice and the restoration of balance in any given situation which calls for forgiveness.

Apart from my own experiences related to the power of forgiveness, I have seen in others the miraculous changes that can be brought about by the act of forgiveness. One such example comes to mind; an associate of mine was robbed of a small fortune by a business partner. He explained his disbelief at what had happened, that he had no inkling that his business partner was capable of such cold-hearted chicanery. The sense of betrayal, the rage, bitterness and hatred that appeared in the victim's heart grew to become a terrible affliction. Within a couple of years of this shock, the burden of his negative emotions had begun to make him sick. An insidious sense of stagnation had also grown to envelop his affairs. As time passed, he realised that he had lost the ability to trust anyone.

With this came the acceptance that he would have to forgive his erstwhile business partner in order to set himself free from what had become an intolerable burden. He confessed that once he found the ability to forgive, his health began to improve significantly and he felt free to get on with his life without the powerful encroachment of bitterness on his thoughts and emotions. Thankfully, he rediscovered his optimism, positivity and a belief in his future. Not long after this, he was even able to take on a new business venture. The change in him was remarkable to see as he had clearly risen up out of the abyss that had claimed him following his business partner's cruel deception.

In this particular case, my associate's business partner disappeared without trace, so I cannot say that he knowingly saw justice done, but he is endlessly grateful for the peace of mind that his decision to forgive has brought him. Even when the law is evaded or is itself unjust, life has its own infallible way of restoring balance. This is very difficult to accept for many people. There are those who offer the fact that so many truly wicked folks appear to get away with the most heinous crimes and die peacefully in their sleep, as proof that there is no Divine Intelligence. If such an entity existed, surely justice would be visibly apparent in the world, whilst history seems weighed down with injustices that have gone unaddressed, and unrepaired. There are those who insist that to the victor go the spoils.

The families that have committed genocide, plunder, deceit and the enslavement of millions seemingly sit atop the heights of power and wealth, as if above all notions of justice. They are even able to rewrite history and paint their crimes against humanity as heroic adventure. We are eternal souls that have nowhere to hide from the justice which life arranges in good time with unfailing precision. Yet this truth is most often veiled from the eyes of the persona believing the patterns and cycles of a single lifetime to be proof of life's indifference to justice.

Furthermore, the persona does not appreciate the innate capacity that your being has to bring perfect justice into play. We need to understand the importance of justice and reciprocity in sustaining balance in the universe and in our own lives. It is crucial, also, to accept that forgiveness is in no way undermined by the execution of justice. If your loved one is murdered in a cold-blooded way by an oppressive regime or a callous individual, you would best forgive the murderer for your own sake but this would in no way cancel the necessity for the murderer to be brought to justice. This necessity would only disappear if the murderer themselves had uprooted the true cause of their violations against life and was therefore willing to redress the balance that has been abused by their actions.

Both on the scale of individual affairs and at the scale of world affairs, the same principle applies. This is why the oppressed, exploited and devastated nations of the world will not receive the reparations they are due unless those that have plundered them abandon the values of the persona (fear, greed, envy, covetousness etc). The lack of justice and reciprocity and the violations of balance which are their fruit are themselves the work of the persona. All political, economic and social panaceas are doomed to fail if this fundamental truth continues to be ignored.

What to do with childhood hurt

Even those who cannot believe that there is more to their being than the body, the mind and a conditioned sense of identity, will accept that there is work we can all do to make our psychological load lighter. Suffering endured during childhood can have a particularly powerful effect on the subconscious mind. Deep-seated negative beliefs that express themselves in later life are often rooted here. Self-limiting behaviours, which sustain insidious patterns of suffering in your life, can emerge as a result. A child who grows up in an environment where they are constantly belittled, put down and made to feel unworthy, may, as a result of this negative programming, grow to be shy, lacking in confidence and to attract relationships which continue the pattern of abuse throughout their adult life. In order to break such destructive patterns created in childhood, it is very effective to deliberately set aside time to look after the hurt child within you.

The following is a guided meditation to help you heal the blocks rooted in childhood trauma:

Take yourself to a peaceful place where you will not be disturbed and make yourself very relaxed. Ideally, listen to relaxing ambient music and take yourself back to your childhood, to the occasions when you were hurt or abused. This will require some courage on your part but your reward will vastly outweigh your sacrifice. Go back to the earliest event of hurt to you and work up towards your adulthood. Each person's journey will be different. You may find yourself being made aware of something that happened to you at age 3, and then age 5, and then age 9, and then age 14; it will be different for everyone, but be assured that you will be shown the events that have made a powerful impression on your subconscious mind and affected your ability to live a fulfilled life as an adult. At each juncture of hurt, suffering and pain that reveals itself, you must see yourself as that child at that age when the relevant event took place and you must take the child's hands and speak to the child. You must comfort and reassure the child and let it know that although it may have been weak and powerless to stop the hurt or abuse that took place then, you are fully grown now and you will look after the child and keep it safe. Tell the child all it needs to hear to know its true beauty and worth. Tell the child that it is intelligent, brave, beautiful and deserving of love and every good thing. Tell the child she or he is a princess or prince of the Divine Presence. With all your heart, give the child comfort and strength, then crucially, forgive everyone who was involved in hurting the child. Forgive them and set the child free by letting the child know that these people no longer have any power over her/him and that the child has been given back all the power that was taken from her/him all those years ago. Forgive yourself (the child) for all feelings of powerlessness and victimhood. End of meditation.

This particular type of forgiveness work is extremely effective at breaking negative patterns in your life that have been created by childhood trauma/abuse. However, all modes of forgiveness work that tend the wounds of the persona are merely clearing a path to the transcendental form of forgiveness that addresses our fundamental problem in this life: our ignorance of our true and Divine nature. When we forgive ourselves for this ignorance, we forgive ourselves for everything and move towards liberation.

This is an internal operation

Your responsibility and your purpose here is to transcend your own persona and live in the glory of your true Divine nature. This is the greatest thing you can do for the whole creation. In the most profound sense, the whole existence is only here because you are here. In ways that are beyond the capacity of words to reveal, your awakening to your true nature affects the whole existence. All that I can say is that you and your significance to the Divine scheme of things are more than your mind could ever evaluate.

Forgiveness helps to clear the mist of forgetfulness that stands between you and your true Self. So, forgive yourself for any wrongs that burden your conscience. Guilt is a grave companion. People with guilt complexes sabotage themselves. They display self-destructive behaviour even when their guilt is not truly justified. For example, some parents feel guilty when their children grow up to be dishonest, dishonourable and unsavoury people despite their best and most sincere efforts. Such parents have no right to be afflicted with guilt since they have not failed to fulfil their role as parents. It may be more just to surmise that the seeds of virtue they attempted to plant in their children fell on stony ground. Society is often swift to blame the parent for the sins of the child and to judge the child by the deeds of the parent but we must free ourselves of such unwarranted blame and any associated sense of guilt.

For those whose guilt is justified, forgive yourself once and for all time. Pay reparation; that means do something to restore balance. Seek inner guidance as to how to best do this and, of course, cease from committing crimes against life. In some cases, it may be impossible to repair the damage done to an individual or their family, but you will give reparation to the creation itself when you transform your behaviour from destructiveness to creativity that serves the community and the creation as a whole. Then your guilt would have served its rightful purpose and be ready to depart your company and leave you free to live in a manner worthy of your authentic Self. Abiding in Awareness is the way to lead such a blameless existence.

Awareness is also the key to understanding which unforgiven issues are blocking your progress or making you sick and how this may be happening. Once Awareness has provided you with such clarity, you can start to discern the beautiful gifts the universe has always been dispensing so generously to you throughout your life. You will also receive a sense of the stupendous blessings yet to come, due to the awakening of the power hidden within you. The faculties, which are the means by which that power is expressed, will also come sharply into focus.

Most important and fundamental of all is the need to forgive yourself for all the years you have spent living under the illusion that you are your persona. This is the root cause of every error you have made, every wrong deed you have ever committed. So, forgive yourself for this and you forgive everything. Your true nature does no wrong, so forgive yourself for living in ignorance of your true Divine nature and you forgive yourself in the most complete way.

Once you have forgiven yourself in this way, with this deep understanding of the cause of all your errors, you can much more easily forgive those who have wronged or hurt you. The cause of their erroneous behaviour is exactly the same as yours; living in ignorance of the Divine nature that is our authentic identity. Those who have wronged you, hurt you or abused you have done so because they have genuinely forgotten who they are. They are not pretending; they genuinely do not know or believe in their own

Divine and supremely peaceful nature. This ignorance leads people to be driven by fear, greed, envy, jealousy, malice, hatred, deceit and a host of other unseemly motivations which produce so much suffering and pain in the world.

These motivations and their fruit of suffering and pain are the legacies of the persona. If you can forgive yourself for your entrapment in the illusory worldview of the persona, you can forgive everyone else, since we have all been similarly trapped to varying degrees. Never forget that even the most heinous criminals are not pretending to have forgotten that they are Supreme Peace. They truly believe that they are lost, abandoned by grace, fighting for supremacy in a ruthless, pitiless world that only rewards those who can act unhindered by scruples or tender-heartedness. They are not pretending; their behaviour is the sure proof of their deeply held belief. Looking at yourself and others in this way will enable you to more readily and easily forgive others since you forgive them for the same error that has held you prisoner all your life.

Forgiveness meditation:

In addition to the childhood work suggested earlier, practise the following meditation for forgiveness and cleansing so that your heart becomes as light as a feather:

Gently relax your whole body and mind. Let go of all tension in your body and let go of all unease in your mind. Free yourself from all tension and completely relax. Look at every cause for regret. Look at every burden you could blame yourself for. Get a clear picture of the things about yourself or the things that you have done which make you feel guilty, all the things regarding yourself which burden your heart. Now, look deeply into the fact that each and every one of these things are the fruits of your persona or ego/self. Every single one of these things that burden your heart with guilt and/or regret belong to your illusory sense of self, your persona, your conditioned self. Accept that none of these feelings, or the actions which gave birth to them, have to do with your true and natural state of peace, freedom and awareness. Simply decide to forgive yourself once and for all for the root cause of all your errors, faults and crimes against yourself, against others, and against life itself.

Just say to yourself, 'I sincerely and completely forgive myself for every day, every moment I have spent in ignorance of my true and Divine nature and I forgive myself for every wrong thought, feeling or act that I have brought into being as a result of this ignorance. I forgive myself now, once and forever more. I abandon ignorance and affirm my decision to abide in my true nature as Supreme Peace, as Love, as Awareness. I rejoice in this freedom, this shedding of every burden, this new lightness and pureness of heart.

Now, just as I have forgiven myself, I can forgive everyone else who has hurt me or harmed me, abused me or exploited me. I forgive them all, now and forever more. I sincerely and completely forgive them as I have forgiven myself, because I know their crimes were borne of the same ignorance that created mine, the ignorance of their Divine nature. Just as I forgive myself, I can forgive them all and bless them with the prayer for their awakening to the wonder of their own true nature. I rejoice in this freedom, this shedding of every burden, this new lightness and pureness of heart. I rejoice in the bringing of perfect justice and the restoration of balance in every situation. We are all returning to equanimity in the Divine scheme of things.'

Repeat this process as many times as it takes for your heart to feel as light as that feather. How long it will take to experience the desired change will be different for everyone; some people may feel a great sense of release and freedom immediately, whilst others may have to repeat this process over a number of days, or even weeks, to experience the definite shift in energy that marks the effective shedding of your heart's heaviness.

Having forgiven yourself in this fundamental way, you must affirm your freedom from ignorance and its bitter fruits. Abide as your true Divine Self and you will have no need to collect any further burdens with which to load your heart. Instead, fill your heart with peace, love and gratitude.

Having forgiven others, accept them as they feel they are. Do not think that you need to be close friends with those who continue to abuse you. They will make their own transformation in their own time, but it is not your role to volunteer for any further abuse whilst they make their way.

A fundamental shift

The feeling of clarity, peace and freedom which arises as a result of this work is distinct and is the proof that you have truly excavated the roots of the negativity which lays claim to our consciousness when we neglect to forgive ourselves and others for all that has caused us pain, anguish and suffering.

Your true nature has never been burdened, ever, by anything that we experience on this plane, so, in reality, it is the persona that is blessed by this process, so that it is available to work as the vehicle of Awareness, Divine Intelligence and Grace here on earth. Your greatest purpose is to abide as Awareness, as Supreme Peace even whilst you face all the drama and challenges of life. However, as long as you inhabit your body, your persona will be expressed. When the persona is devoted to the Divine Self, it becomes the means of Divine expression on this plane of existence. In this state, the persona works in harmony with the Divine Presence to bring all our faculties into operation in our lives to fulfil our practically limitless potential. Healed by its ignorance of the Witnessing Presence, the persona becomes the servant of the Divine Will rather than the antagonist that has covered the world in pain and misery.

The more you abide in your true nature, the more the need for forgiveness work will fade into insignificance since the sublime nature of Awareness transcends the scenarios which would previously have wounded your heart or brought you low. The magnificence of your natural state will truly set you free from the traps set for your ego/self.

Living under the delusion that you are the persona has you experiencing only the top soil of life's fathomless depths.

Awakening to your Divine nature, to Awareness itself, begins your journey into a mystery, a joy, a peace and bliss that defies any attempt at description. Here, you begin to realise the infinitesimal nature of all your suffering, of all human suffering, in relation to the limitless Grace, Power and Love that exists at the source of Being and that we are inseparable from that Source.

Our suffering is relative to the Bliss that is our true nature in the same way that time is relative to eternity. We are, indeed, eternity dreaming time just as we are Bliss dreaming pain. To awaken from our dream is to know the Truth and experience the boundless beauty of Reality, Reality being the unchanging source of existence as opposed to the ever-changing phenomena that make up our experience of life. Awaken to your true nature, become established in Reality and you become a lucid dreamer. Engage with life fully, live life to the full whilst you are here, but do so now from the source of Being, as the Witnessing Present, fully engaged but sublimely detached, free of all suffering and delusion. To live like this is to restore health, joy, peace and prosperity to your life and that of the whole world.

Living as a recluse, hiding from the chaos and suffering in the world, shunning the secular nature of the modern world has its own value but is not proof of our Divine nature. Living fully awakened to your true nature in the midst of the world's turmoil is proof of being established in your rediscovery of the Self. Though this life is indeed a dream, it is to be taken most seriously and dreamt lucidly, lest your search for Truth leads you into dangerous delusion and even disaster. Be fully present, here and now, your feet firmly planted on earth, yet, in each moment, cognizant of your true, pristine and eternal nature and abiding, as Awareness opens the way, to the full use of the faculties intrinsic to your being.

In the coming chapters, we will look at these faculties in detail. We will also look at the ways in which these faculties can enrich your life here on earth rather than in some promised heaven to come. Yet still, the awakening of your true nature and the faculties through which it can find expression is the surest guarantee of an auspicious progression to the subtle realm once your time here has come to an end.

Chapter Three: Power

The importance of power

The question of power is central to how we experience our lives. It is fundamental to the quality of life we are going to enjoy here. In the most basic sense, each cell in your body requires power to function. We need power in order to breathe. In order to exist, your body must harness the mysterious power that affords life. We need power (energy) to accomplish our most cherished desires, but we need power in order to meet even our most basic needs and to fulfil our responsibilities. So, the question of power leaves no-one out. To be powerless puts your very survival at risk.

The word power itself often conjures notions of the might wielded by the few who have accumulated mind-boggling wealth, influence and the means to manipulate the destinies of nations and humanity as a whole. Talk of power, thus, most often inspires ideas of dominance and influence over the lives of others using economic, political, social and military means. This is the power the persona seeks to sate its fear and it's deep-seated sense of insecurity. Indeed, it is this arena of power-seeking that has brought the world its incalculable toll of death, destruction and suffering. It is from this realization that the idea that power corrupts and absolute power corrupts absolutely arises. This is such an enduring and prevalent idea that many of the people best suited to positions of power and responsibility shun the opportunity to assume such positions due to the strength of this belief (often held at a subconscious level). However, the power we speak of here is not the power sought by the persona, but the power residing at the source of Being. This power is available to us all and this power perfects you rather than undermining your integrity in any way. This is the power that liberates the soul rather than imprisons it. This is the power that purifies and uplifts your whole being.

Never doubt the Absolute nature of this Divine power that surpasses the power sought by men to dominate and control others. The nature of the world we live in today requires each person to seek genuine empowerment. The persona has fashioned a global system of parasitical exploitation that has rendered the majority of the world's population poor and tremendously disempowered in the social/economic/political sense of the word. Even in the most technologically advanced and wealthy societies, the majority of the populace have been reduced to the status of debt-ridden wage slaves who are encouraged by the most sophisticated and underhanded means to be consumers rather than empowered citizens who would play the decisive role in their own destinies.

As technological developments of staggering significance enable those holding the levers of power in the world to pursue overarching surveillance, manipulation and control over everyone on this planet, there has never been a time in human history when the individual citizen has been more in need of the fathomless power that lies at the source of our own being. This power is available to us all, regardless of status, gender, race or creed and is the infallible defence against those that would render you a mere pawn in their game of dominance and control. The power intrinsic to your own Divine nature is not malleable to the machinations of the persona, either on the individual or collective plane. This is your defence against the power the persona, in its ignorance, holds so dear. This innate power of yours is also the means to living an auspicious life even in an age of decadence, degradation and deceit.

The price of powerlessness

To remain ignorant of the power residing at the depths of your being is to risk being a helpless victim of those claiming power and authority over you, often without your consent. When you discover the power of the Divine Presence within you, there will be no greater authority with whom to consult regarding how to live this life on earth. Throughout history, people have committed the most heinous and evil acts because they have relinquished their responsibility to choose between right and wrong to the authority that issued an order. Thus order-followers have covered themselves in blood whilst the masterminds remain far from the carnage involved in the implementation of their ideas. No-one who comes to know the power residing in the depths of their own soul would assume the role of thoughtless order-follower. The men who dropped the atom bombs on Hiroshima and Nagasaki committed a heinous crime against humanity and the natural environment, on the orders of their government, and would be every bit as responsible as those who fashioned the orders that brought the destruction, pain and suffering unleashed by those bombs. Living in harmony with your Divine nature liberates you from the criminality intrinsic to the issuing or following of such orders.

You may not be a thoughtless order-follower but the sense of powerlessness so commonly felt in the face of the persona's machinations can be equally disastrous. Acquiescence in the face of manipulation, psychological intimidation, persecution or physical force brings the harvest of powerlessness that the persona fears so much yet produces with such fecundity. The persona's lust for power is the root of the powerlessness felt so keenly by so many, even in our technologically advanced age.

Authentic power is available to everyone

You need not beg any worldly authority for the most precious power of all; it is your birthright and this power oppresses and dominates no-one. Instead, this power sets you free from suffering, oppression and domination. This power also sets the oppressor free from the need to oppress or dominate anyone.

Without us turning to the Source of our being, the One Awareness, the Supreme Peace at the innermost depths of our souls, for the power to live here, we will continue to poison and destroy that which sustains us here on earth; the land, the sea, the sky and every beautiful thing to be found here in our world. The turmoil, suffering and pain will continue in our personal lives too until we turn inward away from the attachments which hold the persona in a trance. We need to sincerely surrender to the Supreme

Peace within. This is why no amount of accomplishment, wealth and power can bring us the peace our soul seeks because we have not realised that we are that which we seek.

Rich or poor, member of the power elite or indigent, every soul is in need of this Supreme Peace and the infallible, pure and blissful power it confers. Some of the wealthiest and most powerful people on this planet are broken at heart, prisoners of the corrupted power they have sought, just as the poor and dispossessed are often broken by the suffering and humiliation that poverty brings. However, those driven closest to despair are also closest to abandoning the embrace of the persona in favour of the search for their true identity. We live in an age where the catastrophic changes which threaten our world will literally drive people to despair. Nevertheless, to turn within and abide in your true and Divine nature is the answer to the challenges of every age in our existence on this plane.

To surrender to your true natural state of Supreme Peace is to empower yourself across every dimension of your being. You will also awaken your slumbering awareness of the limitless benevolence existing in the universe. This opens you to the wondrous workings of Divine intelligence, which will become more and more apparent in your life, the more sincerely and constantly you surrender to the invincible Peace that you truly are.

Without this ultimate empowerment, we may succumb to the multiple pressures involved in living here as the persona. Many find it impossible to cope and resort to intoxicants to medicate their pain. Some people find themselves in such depths of despair that they cannot endure their torment any longer and commit suicide. Without the power to live your life well and to transcend the suffering which comes with a mind and a body, life could end up being very baffling, frustrating and painful. In contrast, the discovery of this power residing within the subtle reaches of your own being, enables you to transcend all life's troubles, challenges and upheavals, replacing pain with unconditioned joy.

The power that comes from abiding as Awareness ignites the powers intrinsic to the various faculties of your being, such as your imagination, your will, your power of belief, your power of love and devotion, amongst many more. These faculties are the means for us to begin to express our Divine nature in our daily lives and they are the tools that enable us to be creative and to shape our lives into forms worthy of celebration and joy. These faculties enable us to engage with life in the most rewarding way possible. Illumined by the Divine Presence within us, these faculties become the vehicle by which miracles can occur in our everyday lives.

No-one then is powerless, though so many people may feel as if they are, confronted with the overwhelming circumstances that can arise in the course of a lifetime. By looking inward to the Source of your own being, you can arrive at the power that is equal to anything life has to present you with. The power found here is distinct from the power being sought and manipulated in the outer world since this power redeems the whole creation and exploits, deceives or abuses no-one, it requires no-one's debasement for its own aggrandisement. This is the power that can do no wrong but this is the power the vast majority of people remain completely ignorant of.

Authority and the power-games the persona plays

Worldly powers constantly demand your acquiescence to their authority. They are constantly insisting you obey even when what they seek of you is totally unreasonable and unjust. However, once you come to the realization of the eternal, infallible power residing within your own soul, you will be free from any compunction to bow to the corrupt authority of the various power mongers demanding that you bend to their will. In an age when the media techniques designed to manufacture the consent of the masses (for any given product or socially desired end) have become so sophisticated, effective and insidious, it is essential to possess the sovereignty of consciousness that the power within you affords.

If it were not for the grace that allowed me to experience this power in my own life, I would not have been able to overcome seemingly insurmountable odds in fighting to save my severely disabled son's life, whilst he endured dreadful abuse and neglect in the care system. Some years ago, my son lived in a care home that saw fit to leave him without heating, in the midst of freezing cold weather and to deny him food. When I discovered the totally unacceptable conditions he was living in, a battle ensued with the care home and the relevant authorities whose job it was to oversee and safeguard my son's well-being. To my dismay, practically all the agencies concerned were far more engaged with protecting their own interests and keeping secure the significant amount of money attached to my son's care package, than they were in upholding my son's safety or well-being. It took two years of legal wrangling with these authorities before the Court of Protection took action that, I believe, saved my son's life. Throughout this battle, I was repeatedly told that I should trust and obey the dictates of the relevant agencies, who insisted that they held the power and authority over my son's fate. They kept insisting that they were the decision-makers and that I would have no say as to what should happen to my son.

These people seemed amazingly confident that it did not matter that my son was literally crying to be removed from the site of his abuse, or that I feared for his life if he remained living at the residential home in question. As this nightmare unfolded, I was told many times by people with years of experience in such matters, that most families in my situation give up under the stress and strain that such abusive and corrupt care homes, and the associated authorities, create in their lives. I came to understand why these agencies were so confident that they would get away with the blatant abuse of their powers, since they all seemed to work in unison to protect whatever arrangements they appeared to have formed together. I received the strong impression that their confidence was based on the probability that they had gotten away with such behaviour many times before.

When I was told I would have to acquiesce to the will of these authorities, I told them the truth, that I did not accept their authority over my son's life or mine. They told me that the Court of Protection would, in time, convince me that I would have to accept their decision regarding where my son would reside in the future. Even my own solicitor warned me that the authorities usually hold sway in such cases, even when the injustice was as clear as it was in my son's case.

Throughout this whole battle, the only reason that I was able to remain immoveable in my quest for justice and to save my son's life, was my understanding that I am the Self and not the persona, given to fear, doubt, anxiety and worry, which would have certainly spelled defeat for me and my son in such a fight. Over and over again, it was suggested to me that I had no right to expect that a simple woman like me could stand against these powerful agencies and hope to win. Nevertheless, I knew at the core of my being that the whole Universe stood at my side, working for justice, because it was the Self and not my persona (or that of anyone else) that was in charge of the outcome. Without going into the details of the court case, a number of miraculous events combined to ensure that justice was done for my son. Crucially, I also know that it was Divine Intelligence itself that arranged for such an experienced, clear-sighted Judge of high integrity to preside over my son's case. It is my conviction that the Self was in charge of those extraordinary events.

My prayer was for justice; I felt in my bones that it was not time for my son's life to end. So, despite everything that I was being told by others, I never doubted that a just outcome would be achieved. This is one example amongst many in my life where my absolute certainty that I am not just a flawed and limited persona has been vindicated by the unfolding of seemingly miraculous events that have combined to save me or mine from the worst.

Live this way

It would be reasonable to ask how you can live in such power that would lift you up above impossible circumstances and bring you victory when defeat seems inevitable. In my experience, the key to living in this power I speak of here, is to arrive at the realization that you are not just your mind and your body, but rather that you are the indwelling Divine Presence that is formless and immeasurable. In order to live in this power, you must know who you are in truth and you must come to understand what you are not. This knowing will grow in you the more you take the time to be still and to let go of all the thoughts, beliefs and conditioning that represent the persona. By abiding in the stillness, the silence, the peace of the indwelling Presence, the conviction will grow that this boundless Divine Presence is your true, immutable, indestructible identity. This Presence holds the power that is equal to any and every challenge that we may meet whilst we journey here, in this cloak of flesh and blood.

This realization can only grow through experience of abiding in this Presence; it cannot grow via any academic exercise. You will only know this when you experience this for yourself. It is not enough to read about it in this book or any other. This book, or any other expressing a similar message, can only inspire you to seek out this experience, this truth, for yourself. You must develop the devotion and the sincerity required to seek this Presence that waits silently beyond your enchantment with the persona.

Turning your attention, constantly and repeatedly, to this Divine Presence within you must become a fundamental part of your life in order for the realization of the Truth about who you really are to become irreversibly established in your consciousness. As this practice becomes your way of life, you will find that you begin to become aware of your persona expressing itself in any given situation. Over time, you will be able to witness the persona with a sense of complete detachment and serenity, so that the persona is no longer directing your feelings and actions. This is a state of liberation and marks the arrival of the power that we have been referring to here.

It is impossible to overstate the importance of beginning to live by the dictates of the inspiration that arrives when you abide as your true nature, rather than by the dictates of society at large which encourages all kinds of desires and intentions which serve some vested interest rather than your own best interest and well-being. We are so much the victims of the conditioning forces in society that we literally do not have minds of our own, but once we return to our true supremely peaceful nature, the way is open for sublime inspiration to arise and shine its light on your path through life. So, the most wondrous power you will ever find resides within your own being. Turn inward sincerely, constantly and you will come to feel this awesome power, eternal, still, boundless, transcendent but so well-hidden in you.

Chapter Four:
Your Power to Choose

The starting point

When we begin to look at how we are going to live, if we are going to fulfil our potential to express our Divine nature here on earth, in this body of flesh and blood, the question of choice becomes crucial. When my spirit left my body and I had accepted my own death, even then, I made the choice to live on. At every juncture in life, we make choices that dictate the course of our lives. The question of choice brings up the mystery of free will, desire, intention and inspiration; these are all facets of the same capacity, our power to choose. This is by no means straightforward territory since the myriad of elements influencing our desires, intentions and choices are many and often unperceivable to the conscious mind. The beliefs held in the subconscious mind powerfully shape the decisions we take in life, often without us understanding how or why. This is why we so often make choices that seem obviously against our own best interest. For example, why would anyone ever smoke cigarettes? The belief held in the subconscious mind that attributes some benefit to smoking has a greater impact on behaviour than the commonly held understanding that smoking kills. In relation to all the faculties of our being, the power to choose has to be our starting point because this is the starting point for the manifestation of the auspicious life referred to earlier.

It is so important to approach this first step on the road to creating better conditions in your life with deep reflection. The choices I made, out of desperation to make it in the rat race in order to provide security for my family, almost killed me. At that time in my life, I was making choices on a daily basis that were self-destructive. If I had stopped to look deeply into what was happening in my life and turned inward to my true nature for guidance and inspiration, I would not have opened death's door under the strain of chasing the goals I had set myself. When we acknowledge the far-reaching consequences that can follow the chain of events set in motion by the choices we make, we will begin to accept the great importance of taking our power to choose into hand and seeking a higher order of understanding and insight to direct us in the use of that power. It was my surrender to the Witnessing Presence that saved my life. That Divine Intelligence, which told me to live one breath at a time, is the same one I have continued to approach for guidance and inspiration when I know I must exercise my power to choose. Since the consequences of our choices can be so grave or glorious beyond description, why leave the power to choose solely in the hands of your persona? It is so often ill-informed and ill-equipped to choose well for your highest good and that of the creation itself; because we are all inextricably linked, each event in the universe has a bearing on every other event in ways our minds can barely fathom. Allowing Awareness itself to be our guide in exercising our power to choose brings us into auspiciousness that would otherwise be inexplicable. This is, indeed, the route to our salvation. Throughout the world's wisdom traditions, the archetype symbolising the Will has been characterized as the saviour/hero figure and this is because the Will has all to do with the power to choose and our salvation does, indeed, rest on how we use this faculty.

The fact that we are not consciously aware of even a fraction of the relevant factors in our environment, never mind the fathomless complexity of the information and beliefs held in our subconscious mind, explains the persona's propensity for making decisions that may address one problem whilst creating ten more. Recent history and its toll of human suffering caused directly by the persona's flawed use of the power to choose is evidence of this reality. The persona's perspective is limited, self-centred, short-sighted, competitive and fear-driven; the fruits accurately represent the tree from which they fall. In contrast, our true Divine nature inspires choices based on the holistic understanding of the world that produces effects that bring balance, harmony and prosperity for us and the whole, of which we are just a part. This is the most profound salvation, sorely needed in an age when the persona has, at its disposal, the means to destroy the world's population many times over and to further devastate the natural world in the process.

Counterfeit desires or Divine inspiration?

When we surrender the power to choose to our Divine nature, our socially conditioned desires and intentions are surpassed by the inspiration we will receive from Divine Intelligence, and yet, still we have the power to choose whether to act on this inspiration or not. This inspiration invariably trumps our ego-driven desires and intentions and provides the vehicle for transformation in our lives and in the state of the world at large.

Many years ago, I experienced a very dramatic example of this dynamic with regard to our power to choose between the persona's intention or higher inspiration. I was invited to go to a boat party in London. At that time, I was living in the Midlands. To be honest, my first feeling on receiving this invitation was one of unease, but I allowed myself to be persuaded to ignore those intuitive feelings. So, the day came when we travelled to London and I found myself on a boat making its way up the river Thames, whilst revellers enjoyed themselves dancing, drinking and socializing.

As the boat made its way through the dark of night, even whilst everyone else was enjoying the party below deck, the feeling of unease returned powerfully. Something told me to go up on deck, to the rear of the boat where I stood transfixed for some while. People came and invited me to re-join the party, offering me drinks, trying to get me into the spirit of the party, however, something told me to stay exactly where I was. After about fifteen minutes, I heard a big bang and the boat received a terrible jolt. I turned around to see that the boat had crashed into a bridge and was stuck, unable to move any further. People who had been standing on the highest part of the boat were thrown off and fell back down onto the main deck of the boat. Panic ensued.

Below deck, people were knocked over and injured by moving furniture. Many of those people sustained serious injuries. Very soon, people began to fear that the boat would sink. Although the emergency services were called, there was no sign of any help arriving for what seemed an endless age. Some of the men on the boat took things into their own hands and began clambering up onto the bridge into which the boat had crashed. These men then began to also pull women up off the boat to safety. This is how I managed to get off the boat and onto the bridge. Eventually, the emergency services arrived on the bridge and a boat arrived to tug our boat to shore so that those left on the boat were also taken to safety.

If I had acted on the initial inspiration I received when I was first invited to attend the boat party, I would never have had to endure that traumatic experience. However, because, as the danger drew near, I did choose to act on the inspiration which prompted me to stand on the deck to the rear of the boat, I escaped injury. This experience helped me to accept the importance of following such inspiration faithfully and I can honestly say that such inspiration has never failed me.

The question of free will

Using your power to choose from the vantage point of your true Divine nature becomes crucial once we understand the degree to which we are, in reality, not acting from free will otherwise. When we leave the power to choose in the hands of the persona, we may believe we are exercising free will when in fact our will is being heavily influenced by external forces, many of which we barely perceive. When I began to understand the powerful influence that astrology has in our lives, I was shocked and experienced feelings of helplessness and despair when I saw how accurately my sometimes-horrific circumstances, from childhood on, were described in my astrological chart. My chart speaks of anyone coming under the forces present at my birth being fortunate to survive childhood with their life intact, which definitely proved to be the case for me. By Grace, I realised that we are, in fact, like a tumbleweed blowing in the winds of fate, until we learn how to transcend every inauspicious influence in our lives, seen or unseen, known or unknown.

The more deeply we look into the course of our lives, the more we can see that we are like players in a theatre production written and directed by someone else. The often painful and tragic course of my own life defied all my best intentions and efforts to realise my dreams of a prosperous, harmonious and fulfilling life. Instead, persecution, malice, injustice and abuse seem to have stalked me since childhood, presenting me with a perpetual procession of horrendous challenges and set-backs. After each heart-breaking disappointment or betrayal, I would dust myself off and try again. I would have said I've borne my cross with a smile, but on reading my astrological chart, I was crestfallen to see that my misery and misfortunes were charted very precisely in the heavens at my birth. Nothing could make you feel more helpless than believing that you are fighting against the hand of fate. This realisation led me to question the concept of free will altogether.

If we are subject to the insidious influences in society, designed to manipulate our will without our knowledge or consent, if we are subject to a million events, ideas or beliefs that infect our subconscious minds without our conscious understanding or agreement, and if the hand of fate seemingly orchestrates all the influences in our lives to produce a story that could be so accurately foretold at our birth, how then can we claim that we exercise free will in our lives? Now, I have come to believe that the only free will we truly have in our lives is the will to choose our true Divine nature over our persona. Only by doing this can we go free and truly transcend all the forces that influence our lives without us even realising what is really happening.

In reality, there is only one choice to make

So, once again, the key to the use of this faculty (The Will, the power to choose) is our connection to our true Divine nature, which is Awareness, The Witnessing Presence, Supreme Peace. By living in constant remembrance of our natural state, we will receive the inspiration which constitutes the correct choice or decision in every instant, but, first of all, and perpetually, we must use the power of choice to choose our Divine Nature over the persona/egoic mind. We must use free will to choose to abide in our true nature and we must equally use our free will to act on the inspiration that arises from our Divine Nature (Divine Intelligence). This is how the faculty of the Will plays its part in creating an auspicious life for you, even in the midst of the turmoil and decadence that marks the present day. In reality, there is only one choice or decision to make that will dictate the nature of all the other choices you make and the nature of the life you will experience here and that choice is to identify with your true nature or to identify with the (illusory, conditioned and fleeting) persona. On this decision rests your ability to fulfil your potential to use the powerful faculties at your disposal to fill your true place in the scheme of things. You will, thus, come to remember the bliss that you are.

Chapter Five:
Belief

The power of our subconscious beliefs

Our beliefs play a critical role in how we experience and live our lives so the understanding and wise use of this faculty is one of the major factors contributing to our potential to live the victorious type of life we have been talking about here. Once again, as with the Will, our beliefs are subject to influences we are sometimes barely aware of. Ironically our subconscious beliefs are the ones that shape our behaviour, much more so than our consciously held beliefs. This is why human behaviour is so often contradictory and totally inconsistent with our professed beliefs. This is why we can intellectually know and believe something but behave in ways that undermine that belief completely. Our dilemma becomes very serious once we accept the tremendous power our subconscious beliefs have to affect our lives.

There is a level at which belief itself (regardless of what is believed in) can create apparent miracles. The placebo effect in medicine is well-documented but the expansion in research that may throw light on the potentially enormous benefit to our health is subject to the massive commercial interests that embody the pharmaceutical industry. Many people reading this would have had their own remarkable experiences of the placebo effect or the effect of having a conviction that something would heal them or solve their problem when, in fact, the thing believed in possessed no such capacity, but the miracle was wrought by the power of belief itself.

It can happen that this realization is arrived at after some time, when previously unknown facts are revealed that leave us in no doubt that it was our belief that we would get the desired result that brought a transformation rather than what we had pinned our faith on. So, the importance of holding a positive belief cannot be overstated. The placebo effect and remarkable instances of faith-healing illustrate the power of suggestion and the power of the mind (once it accepts a suggestion) to make that suggestion come true. In this context, what you believe in is less significant than the fact that you wholeheartedly believe. It is obvious that we must master this faculty and make sure to mould our belief system into the most positive shape possible lest we create havoc for ourselves with patterns of negative beliefs that will render us sick, poor and dejected. This power of belief works with equal power positively or negatively to bring circumstances into our lives that reflect our deeply held beliefs. To achieve such mastery is no small matter since we are, due to the nature of the subconscious mind, often unaware of the beliefs that are behind our behaviour and the patterns we see repeatedly occurring in our lives. It will often take therapy or inner-child work (as referred to in chapter two) to unearth the beliefs that may be undermining our progress in life. It takes courage to do this kind of work, since it can be painful to face up to the events that have wounded and scared us and then created deep-seated, negative belief patterns. We also carry many negative beliefs passed on to us by our families, our religions, the media, the education system and society at large.

Take our beliefs about money as an example

Examine your beliefs about money, for example, and you may observe the tremendous amount of negativity that has been suggested to you since childhood with regard to money. As a result, the vast majority of people have an uncomfortable and often painful or conflicted relationship with money. This is surely why, at a time in human history when there has never been such stupendous wealth as exists today, so few people experience financial freedom in their lifetimes. Notwithstanding the inequities and injustices of the present-day global money system, it is our deeply held beliefs about money that dictate the nature of our relationship to it.

The love of money is the root of all evil; it is easier for a camel to pass through the eye of a needle than for a rich man to enter the kingdom of heaven; money does not grow on trees; filthy rich; filthy lucre; money does not come easy the list of negative sayings about money goes on and on and if we add to this list all the films, books and plays that reinforce the impression that riches are powerfully associated with corruption, ruthlessness, callousness and greed, it is not difficult to see how your subconscious mind could build beliefs about money that may sabotage your chances of having a healthy, positive relationship with money. Having been fed such a diet of negative impressions regarding money since childhood, you could easily take the stance, even subconsciously, that riches are so tainted that you will forgo them because you are not willing to take on the unseemly attributes they seem to require in those that seek riches, or you could conversely decide to become, callous, ruthless and unprincipled because this is what is required to be wealthy. Both these sets of belief would be erroneous but it is easy to see how young minds could be thus affected by the negativity that is so commonplace in relation to money, so that both rich and poor can end up with a poisonous psychology regarding money that sows the seeds of so much misery in the world. The fact that the negative attitudes to money, wealth and riches that hold sway in society arise from the persona's acute, fear-driven sense of insecurity and lack is highly significant and warrants closer attention towards the end of this chapter.

However, for now, observe your deeply held beliefs about money and see if they are reflected in the reality of your financial status. What were you told during your childhood about money? Did you experience lack and financial hardship? What beliefs did your experiences create in you? Making this close observation of your own beliefs in relation to this one aspect of your life and acknowledging the relationship between your beliefs and your present reality will convince you of the tremendous significance of the beliefs we hold in our hearts and the power of those beliefs to shape our reality.

Taking inventory

We could make a similar inventory of our beliefs with regard to our health, our relationships or our careers and a similar faithful correlation between our deeply held beliefs and the outcomes we experience in our life would become apparent. You will thus appreciate the power and importance of mastering this faculty. If I look at my own life and use my relationship with men as an example, I can see clearly how my deeply held beliefs played out in my life and produced situations that reflected and reinforced those (in this case) negative beliefs. I have to confess that by the time I had reached my early middle age, I had decided to cease even thinking of seeking any friendships with men, such was my weariness with the abuse and disrespect I had suffered at the hands of men professing to want to be my friend or partner. I genuinely felt happier with the idea of being alone than being involved with men who seemed so at odds with themselves that they could not give the love, care or support I felt that I deserved (since I was so giving myself).

I came to acknowledge that my childhood relationship with my father had created subconscious patterns of belief that would come to shape the nature of relationships I would have with men. I began to see that the correlation between the nature of my childhood relationship with my father and what I would experience in relationships as a grown woman was scarily apparent. This insight, however, only arrived after the persistent encouragement of female friends insisting that I could not give up on relationships at my age. Everyone else seemed far more concerned about my situation than I was. From my own perspective, I was very happy in my own company, and I was enjoying my solitude, taking the time to deepen my relationship to spirit. My friends did eventually succeed in getting me to go out, where I met a handsome, highly intelligent man from my community who wanted me to go on a date with him. It suffices to say the disaster that followed (replete with the disrespect and abuse that has faithfully kept company with my relationships in the past) was enough to stop me in my tracks and force me to examine what was happening in my life. Why was I constantly meeting men who behaved in these ways no matter how promising they may have appeared at the outset? I was forced to look at my beliefs about men and my relationship to them.

I began the process of looking deeply into my past, starting with my relationship with my father, and I saw definite similarities between the relationship I had with my father as a child and my adult relationships with men. I looked closely at those adult relationships and had to confront the emotions those relationships evoked and the beliefs that were formed as a result. This was how I came face to face with the degree of resentment and mistrust that had built up inside me, especially towards the men in my community to whom I naturally looked for love, respect, support, solidarity and a sense of togetherness and common purpose (which I felt was common-place in other comparable immigrant communities in the UK), only to be disappointed in so many varied and painful ways.

I realised that it was no wonder that I repeatedly attracted men who proved to be unsuited to me since I had unconsciously developed such a negative pattern of beliefs concerning my relationship with men. It came to the point where I decided to cease even looking for a relationship, and instead, concentrate on transcending my negative beliefs about men. How could I attract positive relationships whilst holding on to such deep-seated fear, mistrust and resentment regarding the male behaviour I was seeing all around me in my community? I saw the clear need to transform my beliefs about the men I would look to for love and companionship. I began by testing my negative beliefs against my life experiences and I found that I could remember, without difficulty, many instances when men had shown me care, love and compassion.

I remember an instant during my early childhood when a senior male family member literally saved my life at great risk to his own safety. I remembered when I was too weak to even walk that it was a male friend (someone society would cast as an outlaw) who showed me the greatest kindness, compassion and care. It was a group of men from my community who gave me tremendous support in caring for my severely disabled son at a time when it would have been very difficult for me to have managed alone. There were many instances, in fact, where men had shown me and my children kindness and support to the extent that my negative belief pattern could not remain intact in the face of the truth from my past.

I did the work of forgiveness regarding the men who had brought pain and disappointment to my door. I also acknowledged the love and brotherly support I had received from men in my community in the past. The end result of this work was my affirmation of love for men rather than mistrust and disdain. I made no attempt to seek a partner even after doing this work on my beliefs. Instead, I handed the issue over to Divine Intelligence to arrange my highest good with regard to a companion.

It is clear to me now that my negative beliefs about men were the work of the persona, just as the negative behaviours I observed with men in my community were the work of the persona. By surrendering this issue to my Divine Nature, I opened a portal for the higher power in our lives to bring order, harmony and balance out of chaos. And so it proved in the most undeniably miraculous way. I was to meet a partner who was, in many ways, a reflection of myself.

This personal experience is just one example I could highlight from my own life to illustrate the inescapably powerful role that our patterns of belief play in shaping our reality. Having accepted the role our beliefs play in our lives, we can also accept the pressing need to master our beliefs so that they produce results in our lives that enhance our well-being and that of those around us.

The foundation for all our beliefs

The foundation from which the work with this faculty must take place is the same foundation required for all the other faculties we will be looking at. It is the theme that must run like a golden thread throughout this book. The foundation we speak of here is based on our understanding of the distinction between our persona and our Divine nature. As we have seen with the Will, when we leave our powerful faculties in the charge of the persona, the persona's ignorance and delusional perspective on reality lead to the toll of sorrow and pain we see in our individual and collective experience of life here on earth. In contrast, to surrender our faculties to the Higher Self, our Divine nature, we find each faculty being inspired and used by Divine Intelligence, the Awareness that is cognisant of everything and acts for our highest good and that of the whole.

So, how do you surrender the mastery of your beliefs to your Divine Nature? You do this by transforming your belief system in one go by concentrating on the one fundamental belief that creates all the beliefs you will ever hold concerning your own life, and that belief is the one that defines your true identity. If you believe you are your body and mind, your memories, your persona, this belief will shape your reality in the way that is common to the vast majority of humanity, with its fruit of suffering, pain, lack and limitation, fear and frustration. However, if you arrive at the conviction that, in truth, you are Divine Nature and know that you are the one single Awareness, the Single Witness of all things, that you are Supreme Peace, eternal, immutable peace and bliss merely dreaming the experience of duality, then your belief system takes a radical transformative shift that puts you in a new illumined relationship with life and the whole creation. Now, you do not merely shape your beliefs in order to improve the conditions in your life; now, you appreciate Being itself as the most wondrous miracle. Now. every moment is a miracle and you realise the sacredness of Being itself and that you are that.

The liberating Truth

So, to return to our observations about our beliefs around money, the persona's beliefs about money are invariably rooted in fear, insecurity and a deep sense of limitation and lack. Some of the richest people in the world have been driven to accumulate mind-boggling wealth due to a strong fear-driven sense of competitiveness that has become insatiable. They feel there is a limited supply of resources and that they must corner it all for themselves if they can. The poor suffer the same belief in limitation and the competitive nature of the arrangements for the distribution of seemingly scarce resources, but they despair of their chances in the race for the money or goods they need. So many people come to believe the playing field is not, and has never been, even. Many inwardly accept poverty and the humiliation that accompanies it as their lot in life. Both of these extremes are polar opposites of the same perspective based on the persona's fear-driven belief system and approach to life. This is the root to the often cruel, viciously competitive and exploitative methods of wealth creation that have fashioned so much misery in the world. All of this feeds the negativity that is thus attached to money, a vicious cycle, a trap within a trap.

What would your Divine Nature, your true, original and natural identity, believe about money? Your true nature knows itself to be eternal opulence. It has, throughout all eternity, been opulence and it will continue to be boundless opulence forever more. Your true nature knows that the persona is merely dreaming, lack, limitation and a vicious scramble for resources that continues its immeasurable toll of suffering for people around the world. Your true nature knows that genuine sustainable wealth arises from creativity which meets our needs here and brings mutual benefit to all. Wealth created joyfully without exploiting, subjugating or deceiving anyone is true wealth, a joyful, beautiful thing; a natural thing seen everywhere in nature, abundance, fecundity, generosity, creativity; it is the natural order of things. Your true nature, therefore, has no guilt associated with its opulence since it is merely an expression of its Divine nature to be prosperous in every sense. Your true nature is free of the fear that stalks the persona and drives it to commit all manner of crimes against its fellows and against life itself in order to attain the status and security wealth promises to bring in the persona-built social order we presently have on earth.

Once more, the distinction between your persona and your true, Divine and eternal nature is the crux of our discussion here. Your Divine Nature will not suffer the fear, anxiety and despair that often surrounds the persona's beliefs and behaviour with regard to money. Your true nature will allow you to rise above the scramble for money and resources knowing that your true nature is that from which all money and resources emanate. Your true nature can suffer no fear of lack. Your nature is one with the source of Being itself and the source of Being is the source of all supply.

Can you see how from this standpoint it is impossible for your true Self to replicate the misery the persona has arranged in the world, for both rich and poor, due to its negative beliefs about money? Such beliefs only reflect the persona's ignorance of our true nature and the sublime Reality which underlies our existence here. If you are able, then, to constantly remember and abide with your true nature, there will be no fear or anxiety, no pride or arrogance, no resentment, envy or jealousy regarding money. You will be at peace knowing that you are naturally opulent in money and every good thing, in all the riches of life, being one with the source of all supply. You will not waver in this belief no matter what your present material circumstances may be. You know that your persona is dreaming a life of challenges and suffering but this dream is a fleeting thing against the eternal Reality of your true and pristine nature.

Hold constantly to the belief system aligned to your true nature and miracles will arrive here in your dream of duality to confirm the veracity of your eternal opulence. Dwell constantly on the feeling of your true nature and it will unfold its full expression in your life here on earth, regardless of the economic climate or any other variable that has been set by the persona's individual and or collective mindset. Your true nature has the power to transcend even the cycles of change that affect every phenomenon in this dimension of life. And be assured, your opulence thus expressed will not be at anyone's expense; rather, it will be of great benefit to the whole creation.

Putting yourself in a state of constant remembrance of your true nature will ignite the tremendous creativity that is an attribute of your original and natural state. In turn, this creativity will produce the avenues and means for your natural opulence to begin to actualise on this plane of existence.

This perspective on the significance of our persona's beliefs compared to the beliefs which accompany our true Divine nature would apply just as well in relation to our health or any other facet of our life. So, in looking at the faculty of belief and how we utilise the awesome power of belief in our lives (to our benefit or detriment, according to the nature of the beliefs we hold) we must address the fundamental question of our true identity and ask who is operating the beliefs that are shaping our lives? Our illusory sense of self (fleeting, fear-driven and ever-changing), or our true Divine Nature (eternal, unchanging, Supreme Peace, Bliss and Opulence)? Mastery of this vital faculty of belief, therefore, comes with surrender to our Higher Self, our Divine Nature. This is the key to harnessing the power of belief in the most complete and beautiful way. This surrender and the mastery of belief that follows will transform your life beyond all expectations.

Chapter Six: Imagination

The vehicle for transformation

The human imagination is a truly amazing faculty that, as much as any other, gives us a clear indication of our essentially Divine nature. Look around at your environment now and you will see the numberless products of the human imagination. Before a chair, a car, an institution or a nation was built, it was first formed in the imagination of an individual or a group of people. We have this wondrous capacity to visualise our desires and then bring them into existence on the material plane. This capacity is hugely unappreciated by most people although we are all using it to powerful effect at all times. The huge problem is that this capacity is being used in an unconscious way, more often to bring the things we fear into being rather than the things we desire.

Our imagination has tremendous power to impress our subconscious mind which has such an unassailable influence on our behaviour and thus on the outcomes we experience in life. Our imagination, coupled with our belief, has the power to condition our subconscious mind to bring us the things or circumstances we desire.

In recent years, there has been an explosion of interest in the Law of Attraction but many people have poured scepticism on the idea that you can visualise something and have it magically appear in your life. Many of these people say they have tried the prescribed visualisation techniques and they most certainly have not worked for them. As I have said, we are all using this faculty at all times to powerful effect, there is no doubt that our capacity to visualise things or circumstances bring them into being in our lives but the alignment with your deeply held, subconscious beliefs is crucial in order for you to manifest your vision. For instance, if you religiously visualise yourself being in perfect health or becoming fabulously wealthy but you have a deeply held subconscious belief that you do not deserve to have perfect health or to be fabulously wealthy, your vision will not materialise until you excavate and replace your negative belief with one that is in perfect harmony with your vision. Without addressing the subconscious beliefs that may be undermining your attempts to benefit from the remarkable faculty of visualisation, you will meet with the unfriendly face of frustration. However, if you can establish harmony between your conscious intentions, your subconscious beliefs and your vision, you will meet with the shining face of success. When this begins to happen, you may also receive a deeper appreciation of the truly Divine nature of your own being. You may begin to appreciate the truly miraculous nature of our existence. You may begin to appreciate that Divinity is not sitting in the sky beyond the clouds but dwells in you.

Emotional alignment is crucial

The awesome power of the imagination needs to be mastered and harnessed knowingly, although its amazing work can be done with great power and consistency even when it is being used in an unconscious way. This can happen if the person involved is fortunate enough to have been blessed with positive conditioning of their subconscious mind from childhood, combined with a naturally vivid imagination and an aspirational attitude to life. Such people can reap the fruits of this faculty seemingly without effort, even without really understanding how they are doing it. However, for the vast majority of people in the world, the nature of conditions is such that most people have to overcome a considerable number of negative beliefs that have been impressed on their subconscious minds since childhood. Moreover, many people have their naturally active and powerful imagination subverted and suppressed by their own parents, the centres of education and the strictures of society at large. So many children are actively discouraged from fully developing their natural inclination to engage their imagination. As a result, conscious effort is often required to rehabilitate the imaginative capacity that was suppressed during childhood.

For those that feel they have lost the ability to vividly imagine what they would like to be, do or have, there are a number of ways to consciously enhance this capacity. Some people find it very effective to use vision boards, whereby they place photos of the things or situations they desire together as a montage on a board that they regularly look at and use as an aid to imagining themselves in the situation they desire. Watching films that depict the conditions you desire can also be a very powerful aid to your imagination, whereby you see yourself enjoying the desired situation depicted in the film. Many people report miraculous results using vision boards. Just closing your eyes and seeing your desire fulfilled in your mind's eye has proved to be tremendously powerful and effective for people going back through the countless annals of time. It is worthwhile experimenting with different visualisation techniques to find out what feels comfortable and effective for you.

Absolutely crucial to the effective mastery and use of this faculty is the right emotional alignment that supports your visualisation work. Emotional alignment is the means for you to get your subconscious mind to co-operate with your efforts to bring your objective into being. If, for example, you desire harmonious, supportive, constructive relationships in your life but you consistently behave in ways that would sabotage the creation of such relationships, you can be assured that your subconscious mind is harbouring beliefs that contradict your conscious desires. Paying attention to your emotional state of being and creating harmony between your emotions and your vision is the way to dissolve the contradictory beliefs held in the subconscious mind and establish congruence between your vision of your consciously held desires and your subconscious belief about that vision.

In this case, for instance, the vision of harmonious, supportive, constructive relationships would be aligned to feelings of gratitude for the people in your life who are analogous to such a situation. Even if there are no such people presently in your life, nurture the feeling of gratitude for such people coming into your life. Nurture feelings of harmony and co-operation with like-minded people; go deeply into what these emotions feel like, identify them and grow them like plants in the garden of your heart. It is the repeated engagement with these positive emotions which will eventually condition your subconscious mind to cooperate with the creation of your desires. When congruence between your conscious desires and your subconscious mind is achieved, you will be amazed at the ease, elegance and sometimes wholly miraculous ways in which your desires will manifest themselves in your life. Such experiences also serve to indicate the underlying unity of all existence. You can thus begin to appreciate our connection to the universe which is able to produce the most amazing synchronicity in our favour. When we begin to realise the harmony and unity within ourselves, which reflects the reality of the entire universe, we will start to gain an inkling of our true intrinsic power. The power of the imagination to manifest your desires is only the very beginning of realising the true nature of the power and glory within you. The successful use of this faculty will increase your confidence in your potential to realise your purpose here, but the beauty that awaits you beyond this accomplishment is fathomless.

Who does your imagination serve?

The question that must be posed in relation to each of our faculties is particularly pertinent here. Is your imagination to be the tool of your persona or your Divine nature? The answer to this question has a crucial impact on the outcomes we will achieve once we have gained mastery of this faculty. The human imagination has given birth to innumerable wonders in this world. However, so many of these amazing things have brought pain, misery and suffering in their wake because they were born of the persona and its often fear-driven and corrupt purposes. When our imagination is inspired by our Divine nature, then it bears fruit that brings harmony, balance and progress to all. The human imagination directed by the persona has produced so much conflict, division, and destructiveness, even whilst producing so many things which reflect our remarkable genius as the most evolved of the sentient beings (we believe) here on earth. When our imagination is surrendered to our Divine nature, a different order of creation begins to take place. We find ourselves manifesting things and situations which fit effortlessly into the bigger picture around us in ways that defy our intellectual means to understand them. We begin to see that thus surrendered, our imagination serves the whole creation rather than our narrow perception of the world and what is important in it. How then can we surrender our imagination to our Divine nature and escape the confines of the persona's mostly fear-driven desires?

Working from the Field of Peace.

If you look back at 'Awareness Speaks', we are informed there that Supreme Peace characterises our Divine nature. We are told, in fact, that this Supreme Peace is existence itself and that it is the prerequisite for all true success. In order to ensure that we use the faculty of the imagination from the standpoint of our Divine nature or Higher Self rather than that of the persona, we can deliberately establish ourselves in this state of Supreme Peace before we visualise any objective. From this place, our success is guaranteed and the highest good for the whole creation is prioritised.

We may, in the process, receive inspiration that shows us something greater than our original desire, but aligning yourself with the eternal stillness, silence and peace which is your own innermost reality adds immeasurably to your consequent visualisation. Combine with your vision the powerful feelings of joy and gratitude you would experience if your vision was already fulfilled and your subconscious will faithfully bring your vision into reality. If you practise your visualisation just before sleep at night, its access to your subconscious mind is made even smoother. Your affirmative prayers are also another powerful means of impressing the subconscious realm. You must take the standpoint that your desire has already been accomplished, that it is already your reality on this plane of existence. The subconscious realm accepts only that which you feel is true. This mystery is the source of miracles and the key to the power of belief. You must have the conviction that your desire is already a reality. You must constantly engage this feeling since it is this feeling that impresses the subconscious realm along with the vision held in your mind's eye. Using your imagination thus, from the state of Supreme Peace, will bring you the miracles which will so powerfully illustrate to you the truth of your essentially Divine nature.

In my own life, the use of my imagination has brought me outcomes which would defy logical explanation and this is a feature of the work done with this faculty; the remarkable synchronicity that comes into play in the actualisation of your desires. There came a time in my life when I felt the urgent need to uproot my young family and leave my home town to move to London. As a single mother living in social housing, I was told that it would be impossible to get an exchange that would enable me to move to London. I set about using my imagination to achieve my goal. At that time in my life, I had not been exposed to any theories about the power of visualisation, I worked instinctively, or as they say in the Caribbean, I followed my spirit.

Thinking about the house I wanted to live in, I formed a vivid picture in my mind's eye of a three-storey townhouse. I drew a picture of my vision and made a habit of visualising this house every day. Going into the depths of the silence within myself, I would see this house and feel that it was already my home. Despite all the authorities and friends saying it would be impossible for me to find such accommodation in London, given my circumstances at the time, I held the absolute conviction that my vision was a depiction of the reality that would inevitably manifest itself in my life at the right time. I entertained no doubt about this. Aside from sitting down in silence to visualise my new home, I would daydream, looking up at the sky telling myself the sky was the limit and I would see this house in my mind's eye even while my physical eyes were wide open. I also indulged in another version of this behaviour whereby I would look out of my window and conduct my daydream whilst sipping a glass of water. The important thing is that you find practices that you are at home with as long as they powerfully engage your imagination in the desired direction and recruit the absolute conviction that your vision is already achieved so that your heart is full of gratitude for its accomplishment.

At the time of my writing this book, I'm still living in the house I visualised and it did come into my possession through a typically astonishing sequence of events that only the subconscious realm could have co-ordinated. This experience, along with many others, has left no doubt in my mind regarding the truly awe-inspiring power to manifest our desires that this faculty of imagination affords us. With such power comes the need for great conscientiousness, so we must use this faculty wisely. Surrendering to your Divine nature is the guarantee that you will not abuse this power and create undesirable consequences down the line for yourself or others. If you are in doubt about the virtue of your desires in the greater scheme of things, you can leave your desire to one side, go into the silence and simply and sincerely ask the Self to show you the highest good for you and all concerned in the given situation. You will be shown a vision of what the highest good would look like. For me, such vision represents inspiration, and inspiration always surpasses even our best intentions. Such visions often describe completely unexpected outcomes but I've never seen such a vision fail to bring the salvation required.

Chapter Seven:
The Truth About Your Emotions

Your emotions impress the subconscious realm.

In the previous chapters, I have made frequent reference to the subconscious mind. The faculties we have discussed thus far, your Will, Belief and Imagination, all combine to influence what the subconscious will create in our lives. However, without the necessary understanding of the crucial role your emotions play in impressing the subconscious mind, you may unwittingly sabotage your efforts to influence the subconscious to actualise your desires.

Maybe the best way to define the subconscious mind is via its comparison with the conscious mind. The conscious mind (objective realm) is often seen as the aspect of consciousness which makes choices and judgements. It forms ideas and directs the subconscious with its chosen thoughts and emotions. The subconscious (subjective) mind receives these directions and faithfully brings their likeness into the visible world. By virtue of this relationship between the objective and subjective realms of consciousness, every single thing is created. On account of this mystery, we have access to the universe's seemingly limitless potential to fulfil our desires. The subconscious realm does not select or judge; it receives the direction from the objective realm and creates its expression in the world as a woman would bear a child having been impregnated by a man. This process reflects the Law of Gender which pertains to the whole creation. It is the union between male and female principles which ignites the creative process that furnishes existence with things.

The key to the successful impregnation of the subconscious realm by the conscious mind is the emotion involved. Any number of ideas come to mind but only those that have an emotional charge will successfully impress the subconscious and lead to the creation of their like in our lives. Understanding this fact makes clear the importance of mastering your emotions and channelling them purposefully to persuade the subconscious realm to yield its treasures in your favour. For instance, if you wish to persuade the subconscious realm to bring you perfect health, you must, along with your vision of yourself in perfect health, recruit the exact emotions you would feel on having attained perfect health; joy, gratitude, confidence, exhilaration, etc. Powerfully engage the feeling that you have already gained perfect health. The idea of perfect health charged with such feelings cannot fail to impress the subjective realm to produce the perfect health you desire.

The importance of your dominant emotional state

Whilst we may grow to skilfully match our positive emotions with the vision of whatever it may be that we desire, we will only be guaranteed success in achieving our goal if the positive emotions we have recruited are dominant and are not overshadowed in any way by emotions which contradict our desire. We would not succeed in our quest for perfect health, for instance, if we harboured strong fears of ill-health and visions of being sick, and if we constantly complained about all the threats to our health. The most wonderful visualisation in the world and the appropriately positive emotions to complement that vision, would not suffice to override the barrage of negative impressions being sent habitually to your subconscious. Ill-health is bound to win out. In order to secure the desired response from the subconscious realm, your habitual mode of thought and your dominant emotional state must be in harmony with your desire; in this example, they must be conducive to perfect health so that no matter what practices you develop to harness your imagination to actualize your desire, you must also pay great attention to the nature of your dominant thoughts and emotions generally and in each moment. By changing your dominant emotional state into a powerfully positive and empowering one, you will change your life so much for the better.

Awareness and mastery over your emotions

In order to gain mastery over your emotions, you must first become well aware of what your dominant patterns of thought and emotions are. So much of our thinking and feeling is repetitive and unproductive. The persona is typically fear-driven in its approach to life and this stance produces endless streams of negative thinking and feeling which impresses the subjective realm and produces the suffering, pain and conflict we see on earth, which, in turn, engenders more fear, thus sustaining the revolving cycle of negativity.

Making yourself truly still and silent, I mean by feeling the stillness and silence at the core of your own being, you can become the dispassionate observer of your thoughts and emotions. Do this frequently over a number of days and you will begin to appreciate the quality of your thoughts and emotions. You will thus be able to make a truthful appraisal of your dominant emotional state and whether it is supportive of your goals in life. I cannot over-emphasise how important this facet of self-mastery/self-realisation is. Only by gaining this awareness of what you are habitually thinking and feeling will you begin to understand how you have been influencing the subjective realm and how you have, therefore, experienced the outcomes you see in your life. It can be daunting to realize the degree of responsibility you have for your own fate in life, especially when you acknowledge that you have been operating the system, unwittingly in blind ignorance, the whole time. This really is the case for most people on earth. But once you start to appreciate the implications of embracing your responsibility, joy will spring in your heart at the sense of freedom, sovereignty and power that will arise in you.

Once you have allowed the Witnessing Presence within you to show you the true nature of your dominant thoughts and emotions, you will be well placed to begin consciously changing your thoughts and emotions into those that are analogous with your desires.

The significance of suppressed emotions

Whilst seeking to master your emotions, it is vital not to make the mistake of suppressing your negative emotions. Negative emotions that are merely masked or suppressed will, in time, take their effect on the cells of your body, leading eventually to sickness and disease. It is better to express a negative emotion in a safe way than to hold it in, allowing it to accumulate in your system in a poisonous way. Best of all is to watch your negative emotions from the standpoint of the Witnessing Presence. This takes the sting out of such emotions and frees you from their grip. You will increasingly be able to watch them come and go until they no longer have any claim of residency and make space for the positive emotions that will create the things you desire in your life; peace, joy, love, happiness, prosperity and success. These things are all within your grasp and do not require that you dominate or control any other soul. All that is required is that you master your own thoughts and emotions, your own faculties and the doors to the universe's boundless blessings are flung open wide for you.

A word about self-talk and our conversations with others

Using your awareness to observe the nature of your own thoughts and emotions will enable you to acknowledge the great importance of the self-talk in which we indulge. Negative self-talk will feed negative emotions which, in turn, impress the subjective realm to create negative circumstances in your life. If mental self-talk is characterised by negative criticism, judgement and condemnation of yourself and others, the anger, frustration and despair that accompanies such thoughts will act to impress the subconscious mind with their like and the subconscious mind will faithfully create circumstances in your life which will appear to merit yet more criticism, judgement and condemnation. Like attracts like faithfully; this means of attraction accurately defines the relationship between the two aspects of consciousness (objective and subjective). This is why the nature of your self-talk is so vitally important. When you can consciously indulge in positive self-talk consistently, until it becomes your habit, the positive transformation of your circumstances is guaranteed. Self-talk characterised by gratitude, optimism, positive beliefs and high aspirations will produce blessedness and auspiciousness in your life.

The implications associated with your self-talk are matched by those of your conversations with others. The same principles apply, in that the conversations you have with others that create negative emotions in you and/or the other person, can bear negative fruit from the subconscious realm in the same way that your self-talk would, hence the vast importance of gaining mastery over your thoughts, speech and emotions. Gaining this mastery over yourself really will afford you mastery over your experience of life.

You can consciously recruit the type of positive emotions you want to entertain consistently by directing your self-talk. You can learn to magnify the positive emotions that are inspired by positive self-talk. For instance, you can consistently say to yourself, "I feel magnificent" or "I feel perfect health pervading my whole being" whilst consciously engaging the appropriate feeling in your heart. Do not be concerned if the feelings appear abstract to begin with. Persevere in identifying and engaging the feelings that match your desire. In some cases, this exercise may expose how unfamiliar some of us have become with positive and desirable feelings. All the more reason to be dedicated to upholding this simple but powerful practice. The aim is to habitually feel the positive feelings about yourself and about life that will bear wonderful fruits once they are reflected back to you by the subconscious realm. Remember that it is your dominant emotional state that will impress your subconscious mind and shape your life here.

Mastery brings miracles

Looking back at the text of Awareness Speaks in chapter one, we are told to "Let Supreme Peace Love and gratitude be your dominant emotional state of being and you will experience miracles in your life every day". Supreme Peace, then, is the foundation on which to build your dominant emotional state. Supreme Peace is, in fact, your original and natural state of being. Mastery of your thoughts and emotions would find you abiding in this state of peace. This state of peace is the prerequisite for true success, so build your mastery over every desirable emotion on the basis of this peace.

Such mastery would put us in the most rewarding relationship with the subjective realm from whence springs the world of our experiences. When we are able to impress the subconscious realm with feelings that reflect our belief in beneficence, harmony and wholeness, auspicious conditions begin to arrive in our lives to mirror these feelings back to us. The more this happens the more our confidence grows in the reality of the relationship between the two aspects of consciousness (objective and subjective).

We thus grow in the understanding that this is the means by which miraculous transformation can happen in our lives. Now, in your heart of hearts, you begin to know that victory is possible even over what appears to be impossible. Understanding your own being in terms of this consciousness lifts you out of servitude, limitation and fear in the face of any oppressive conditions. A remarkable sense of freedom and power arrives with this understanding regardless of your current circumstances.

Constancy in holding the state of Supreme Peace and adding to that the emotions which reflect your desired outcomes in life guarantees you success, victory, and untold joy. All you need do is give this quest for mastery your sincere focus. Sincerity and constancy are everything; the universe will meet you and guide you to a glorious place if you are constant and sincere. There is nothing in life more worthy of your efforts and attention than this great work of self-mastery. The world is full of the suffering caused by people's attempts to master and control others when really all any one of us needs to do is master ourselves. The rewards of mastery over your own thoughts and emotions are literally boundless and transcend suffering rather than piling it up in the world. Make Supreme Peace your dominant state of being and add to that state the feelings that will attract the good you desire for yourself and others and watch for the wonders that will arrive in your life.

Ironically, the most powerful example of this truth that comes to mind from my own experiences involved the passing of a dear friend. We had discussed the mysteries of life many times during our friendship but it was the arrival of a tragic and ultimately fatal illness that led to her amazing transcendence of her dreadful circumstances and her accomplishment of the mastery spoken of here.

When I heard that my friend was dangerously ill, I went to visit her in the hospital, only to find someone looking like a shrunken shadow of the robust woman I had known her to be. In fact, I did not recognise her when I first saw her on the ward. It was only when I looked into her eyes that I knew it was her. Inwardly, I was shocked and disturbed at her appearance and immediately had cause to fear the worst. Somehow, however, I held my composure and did not display my distress to her. After a very little while, she began explaining her heart-break at the reaction of her immediate family members who had visited her some days before. She said that, on seeing her, they had disintegrated into tears and became completely distraught. "How do you think that made me feel?" she asked me and she expressed her gratitude for me not reacting in a similar manner. This led to a conversation about the state of Supreme Peace which can help us to transcend every challenge. She spoke of her determination to arrive at and abide in that state despite the physical and emotional pain she was enduring. The people closest to her, who she had most expected to receive care and support from, seemed to have abandoned her and couldn't even take the time to visit her in hospital. Somehow, however, she gathered up all her anguish and disappointment in order to let it all go in favour of the Supreme Peace we had discussed together.

My dear friend was as good as her word and she was able to achieve the mastery of her own thoughts and emotions that would bring her peace and liberation from all the attachments that had brought her pain and disappointment. This dear friend passed on within weeks of our conversation, but, in that time, her whole being was transformed as she did indeed arrive at a miraculous serenity even whilst she suffered so much pain. She will forever serve as a great inspiration to me because she became the embodiment of the teaching regarding our original and natural state of being. In her, I saw a humble woman (like myself) become the living and powerful proof of this teaching.

Shortly after her departure from this plane of existence, my friend appeared to me in a vision. She was luminous, surrounded by golden light; she assured me that she was now in a beautiful place and she gave me advice which proved to be precise and invaluable. This dear friend proved to me that this revelation regarding our true nature was not just the domain of ancient sages, saints or philosophers but it is our greatest purpose, regardless of our station in life and that we all have the means within us to accomplish it. My dear friend also proved to me that this victory can be gained even in the face of a tragic and painful death. This victory can be gained even in the face of rejection or abandonment from loved ones or even society at large. In reality, there is nothing closer to us than our true Divine nature and, in reality, we cannot be separated from this Peace that we truly are. Watching my friend turn the dross of a harrowing death into spiritual gold by virtue of her self-mastery confirmed for me, beyond doubt, my own experience of the Supreme Peace spoken of in this book.

The truth about our emotions lights our path to freedom and to the fulfilment of our ultimate destiny, which is to return to our true nature. Here, we inherit the fullness of life and when our time here is done, we can transcend the fear of death. The persona searches the world for power and fulfilment not knowing that what is being sought, in truth, will never be found in the world, before it is found within the innermost depths of your own being. Most certainly, the powerful relationship between your emotions and your subconscious mind opens the door to the accomplishment of every mundane goal and, more importantly, the achievement of your greatest purpose; Self-Realization.

Chapter Eight: The Grateful Heart

How gratitude rescued me from hopelessness

Our capacity to feel gratitude has a truly remarkable power to bring miraculous changes into our lives. At a time in my life when I was at my lowest, it was the practice of gratitude that lifted me out of the abyss that had claimed me. Having worked myself to death's door (as explained in chapter one), I lay on my bed unable to move, watching all my efforts come to nought and all my hopes evaporate, as if I was the victim of a cruel joke. It is hard to describe the feeling of defeat, desolation, frustration and anguish I felt at that time. All of this was happening internally as I could barely raise the strength to move a muscle, such was the depth of my exhaustion. Before I reached the blessed point of surrender to the spirit that began to guide me through this oblivion, the sense of hopelessness enveloping me had become overwhelming and I was, indeed, willing to give up on this life and humbly leave this realm.

It seems it was not my destiny to die at that juncture in my life, having failed to accomplish my humble goals. Subsequent to deciding I was not going to give up on life, I began to follow the inspiration that would cut through the brain fog and disorientation that were amongst the many distressing symptoms of my condition. I began to tell myself that, with each passing day, I would get better and I began to feel a deep sense of gratitude for every incremental improvement in my strength. Taking up this approach to my situation brought into being a wonderful change in my mood and my outlook as a whole. My dire sense of hopelessness was replaced by a growing belief that I would be able to recover and live a worthwhile existence despite the challenges I would have to overcome. The rekindling of hope made all the difference to my perspective on my still-unenviable situation. The more grateful I was, the more my healing progressed. I was sincerely grateful for each and every small improvement I made because things that I had previously taken for granted, such as getting up on my own and walking down the stairs, became a source of great joy and even excitement. My gratitude was deeply felt since regaining each lost capacity was so precious to me. Each improvement increased my faith that the day would arrive when I could once again be independent and self-sufficient.

At the time, I did not even consciously recognise the full power and significance of what I was doing. All I knew was that I was simply following the blessed inspiration that I was receiving in my seemingly hopeless state. Since that fateful time in my life, I have come to more fully appreciate the wondrous power that gratitude has to transform our patterns of thinking and feeling. Based on my own personal experiences, I can say with conviction that, in terms of creating positive changes in our lives, gratitude is amongst the most powerful of all our capacities.

Gratitude and the subconscious realm

There is an infallible reason for the wonder-working power of gratitude which again has everything to do with the relationship gratitude begins to create between us and the subconscious realm. Gratitude has the power to put you in perfect and harmonious relationships with the subconscious realm. The more you practise gratitude, the more your patterns of thinking and feeling will tend towards positivity. The more consistently this happens, the more the subconscious realm will receive impressions which will flower into more and more auspicious conditions in your life. The subconscious realm faithfully creates our experiences of life in the likeness of the dominant patterns of feeling with which we impregnate its limitlessly fertile capacity to shape our universe. How we relate to this realm could not be more important.

To take control of the thoughts and feelings you wish to impress upon your subconscious is to take control of your own destiny. To make gratitude amongst the most dominant of your habitual feelings is to allow the subconscious realm to transform your circumstances in ways that often defy explanation. However, beneath the undeniable mystery central to the operation of the subconscious realm lies the infallible certitude of the law which defines the relationship between our thoughts, our feelings and this realm. The law I speak of here is embodied in the fact that the subconscious accepts whatever we impress upon it without judgement, discrimination or protest. Whatever the conscious mind holds at the level of conviction, the subconscious will set about creating its likeness in your life, regardless of the benefit or detriment that this may ultimately bring to you. The conscious mind must choose carefully what it serves up to the subconscious realm. To make gratitude the nature of your dominant emotional state is to bring the infallible law to your side as an invaluable friend. Practising gratitude must be amongst the easiest and most pleasurable ways to transform your patterns of thinking and feeling. Thus, you will enable the law to work for you rather than against you (which is often the case for so many of us here on planet Earth).

The importance of gratitude for what you have.

Whatever conditions prevail in your life at this very moment represents a reflection of the impressions made on your subconscious mind over time. In many cases, we may not be able to identify the patterns of thoughts and feelings that have produced a particular unwelcome event in our lives, but the law is infallible, so that looking deeply at your life and your dominant emotional states will reveal the link between your internal world and the dramas unfolding in your life.

To begin to master your own thoughts and feelings is to leave unwitting victimhood behind and head towards mastery of your own fortunes in life. The consistent practice of gratitude is a priceless aid to the attainment of such mastery. Many people advocate keeping a gratitude journal as a means of forming the habit of focusing on the things you are grateful for. Any practice that helps you to shift your mode of thinking and feeling towards positivity is to be endorsed, However, becoming aware of your thoughts and feelings in each instant and consciously turning to peace and love as well as gratitude is the path of action I would most recommend. As declared in "Awareness Speaks" in chapter one of this book, this is the means to the complete healing of your woes, on every level of your being. This is so because abiding in the emotional state embodied by supreme peace, love and gratitude effectively dispels all illusions and the negative, limiting beliefs that have previously been impressed upon the subconscious realm. This is the prerequisite for authentic and permanent healing to take place. On the way to this ideal, there are steps that will send us in the direction of such mastery with ever-growing confidence that we can indeed return to our original and natural state of being.

In building the habit of being grateful, a beautiful way to start is to focus on being grateful for the good you have in your life at present. This quickly begins to shift your mindset towards an appreciation of what is good in your experience, rather than dwelling on the undesirable elements in your life. In light of the infallible law discussed previously, the advantages of making such a shift in mindset are obvious. As I explained at the beginning of this chapter, it was the practice of being truly grateful for each increase in the modicum of energy in my body, instead of focussing on my devastating fatigue, that helped me to resurrect myself from the mood of hopelessness and defeat. It did quickly become my habit to look for each increase in my capacities with a sense of celebration and deep gratitude. My health continued to respond positively to this shift in mindset until the time came when no-one looking at me could imagine the degree of ill-health I had suffered, or that I had walked into death's entrance hall only to escape the pull of the fatal hospitality awaiting me there.

My experience provides a dramatic example of what gratitude can achieve for us but this simple act of being truly grateful for what you have rather than bemoaning what you lack works powerfully to change any situation around in your favour. For instance, give thanks for the money you have got rather than telling yourself that you have no money (which only serves to encourage the feeling of lack). We now know what the subconscious realm will produce once you've impressed it with such a feeling. Whereas appreciating and celebrating whatever you have got engenders the feeling of having and the subconscious will equally go to work to reflect this feeling back to you in your objective reality, i.e., you will find yet more money turning up in your life. This applies to all life's riches, thus there could hardly be an easier or more rewarding means of approaching the great work of mastering your own thoughts and emotions. Do all that you can to nurture this miracle-working habit since it is amongst the very best ways to put yourself in the right relationship with the infallible law.

No matter how dire you may believe your situation to be, you can only benefit from turning your mind to the task of finding things to be grateful for. Before you fall asleep at night, think of and give thanks for the things you are truly grateful for; the life in your body, your senses, your loved ones, the roof over your head, your livelihood and so on. Do this consistently and you will discover more and more that is worthy of your gratitude, and we do literally have a whole universe of things to be grateful for. Doing such a mental exercise just before going to sleep helps your ideas to more easily reach the subconscious realm, however, you will be best placed when you can make this mode of thinking and feeling your habit day and night, hour by hour, minute by minute. By such means, you will nurture the grateful heart. Focussing on what you are grateful for and feeling good about it, rather than focussing on what you find undesirable and feeling bad about it, will change your life in ways that will amaze you.

The immense power of gratitude for your desires yet to be fulfilled

Having nurtured the grateful mindset by focusing on and giving thanks for the good you already have in your life, you will be excellently placed to take a further step that will enable you to become the creator of the dreams you hold most dear but have been unable to manifest. Now is the time to discover the power of being grateful for the things you desire but have yet to realise. The key point here is that you must see and feel that your desire has already materialised. So, give thanks and celebrate in your heart just as you would when your desire has become a physical reality. What you believe is true is accepted as fact by the subconscious realm and it creates your objective reality accordingly. Thus, you can appreciate the tremendous power the human imagination has to manifest our desires when placed in the right relationship with the subconscious realm and the infallible law that governs it.

It could be that you long to find yourself well-placed in a job or career that brings you a sense of fulfilment as well as prosperity, but you have never managed to find yourself in that situation. You may, instead, constantly find yourself in employment that leaves you feeling drained and unfulfilled but you feel trapped because you must pay your bills. In such a case, you must drop the discontent and frustration the situation may be causing you to feel, and instead, engender a feeling of peace, love and gratitude in your heart. Think deeply about the situation that would meet your true heart's desire. See yourself as a great success in the job or livelihood you desire for yourself. Think deeply about what you would feel like if your dream was now made a reality; powerfully inhabit those exact feelings and fill your heart with gratitude for your success. By doing this, you will impress the subconscious realm with the idea of your desire being gloriously fulfilled. If you can bring this feeling to the level of absolute conviction, the mysterious operations of the subconscious realm and the infallible law that regulates it will go to work in your favour to bring your long-held dream to fruition.

However, success will continue to evade you if you cannot still the negative chatter of the mind which will clutter the subconscious realm with ideas and feelings that are contradictory to your conscious desires. This is why staying in the state of peace, love and gratitude is so important and lends so much power to your work when you begin to use your imagination and your emotional capacities to build the reality you wish to inhabit for yourself and for the good of all. Miracles will indeed happen when your consciousness is cleared of the negative and limiting beliefs that frustrate all your attempts to manifest your good. Abiding in the state of supreme peace disarms the negativity that so often mires our subconscious mind. Once a state of deep and constant serenity is rediscovered (because this is our original and natural state of being), it becomes much easier to manifest your desires by seeing and feeling that your wish has already been made real. This is just one facet of the awesome power found in the stillness, silence and peace spoken of in 'Awareness Speaks'.

Building the feelings associated with the fulfilled desire to the level of absolute conviction is essential. Harbour no doubt in your heart; instead, feel with absolute certainty that your desire is already made real and it is only a matter of time before it takes form in the physical universe. It is important to note here that the realm of thoughts and feelings (though subtle and often imperceptible) is every bit as real as the physical realm and that everything arriving in a physical form first arises from the subtle realm of thought and emotion. Everything is, in fact, consciousness vibrating at different levels from subtle to gross, from cause to effect. Thus, it is vital to appreciate that your thoughts and emotions are every bit as factual and real as the physical circumstances they eventually create. This is both the crux of the severe challenge that living on this plane of existence can sometimes be and the means for our liberation from suffering.

Once you truly appreciate that your thoughts and emotions held at the level of absolute conviction are equal to the facts that can be perceived with your physical senses, then you will more easily operate the infallible law in your favour, to create a world which reflects your desires for your own good and that of others. Gratitude for the fulfilment of your wishes, even before they have materialised on the physical plane, is one of the most beautiful and effective ways of successfully manifesting your desires for good. Understanding the relationship between your thoughts and feelings and the subconscious realm puts the power of gratitude to open the door to the universe of life's riches into context. Such an understanding will make it easy for you to accept what you would otherwise have deemed impossible. It will become easy for you to see that miracles are, in fact, no more than the workings of the infallible law.

The beauty of gratitude

There can be no more beautiful way to avail yourself of the power of the human imagination in the right relationship with the subconscious realm than the use of gratitude in the way described above. The emotional state of gratitude is amongst the most beautiful and powerful of all the emotional states available to the human heart. It is a shame that so few are aware of its awesome power to improve their lives on every level, since gratitude has the power to bring the human mind into greater harmony with the Divine nature which is our innermost reality. Gratitude has the power to swiftly elevate our consciousness to the level where the lucidity required to discern your own Divine nature becomes available. Thus, your awareness of the power and beauty which pervades existence begins to reveal itself to you and the realisation grows that all the suffering and woes of a million lifetimes on earth cannot diminish in any way the fathomless grace, peace and unconditional joy of the Divine Presence that holds our existence in its loving embrace. Yes, used with understanding gratitude is a powerful tool for manifesting your desires, however, it is also a most wonderful means to deepen your spiritual connection to your eternal and Divine source. Herein lie untold power and untold joy, simply from the constant and faithful practice of keeping a grateful heart. This is a certain means of transforming your life for the better. If you sincerely adopt the grateful heart now, your own personal experiences will be all the evidence you will need regarding the veracity of my suggestions here. Cultivate the grateful heart and you will be amazed at the changes that will begin to adorn your life.

Make gratitude your emotional headquarters

A deep and sincere look at the patterns that have faithfully reoccurred throughout your life's progression will reveal that they reflect the dominant emotional states you have inhabited throughout your life; most especially during your formative years. It is the dominant emotional states, the states felt most deeply and those experienced most frequently that have planted the seeds in the field of your subconscious mind which produce the fruit represented by your objective reality. Understanding the significance of the relationship between our emotional states and the subjective realm puts us in a position of great power if we can begin to take control of our emotions and choose them wisely for ourselves.

There is a widely spread belief that our emotions are essentially our means of responding to our experiences in life and, as such, they are largely out of our control. Our emotions are supposedly shaped by the things that happen to us in life as if our emotions are a reflex response. We are encouraged to express our emotions and not suppress them since this is ultimately unhealthy. It is true that to suppress or repress powerful emotions is to invite ill-health. The body will express dis-ease held within it over time; this is why the roots of many illnesses are to be found in emotional discord of one type or another. It is, for instance, much better to find a safe way to express your anger than to suppress it, which allows toxicity to accumulate in the cells of the body, eventually bringing injury to your health. However, best of all is to develop the control of your thoughts and emotions to the degree where you can calmly choose not to be angry but to remain in your original and natural state of peace, even in the face of provocation. Instead of suppressing anger, you can choose to feel its polar opposite; calm and serenity. You would thus also be much better placed to face the challenge being presented by whatsoever would have otherwise incited your anger. By making gratitude your emotional headquarters, you will find that such control will arise with little effort when it is most needed.

Constantly sustaining the grateful heart will build a powerful spiritual immune system against the negativity that undermines our happiness, health and prosperity. The fact that this practice is so pleasurable and potently effective makes it amongst the very easiest ways to establish mastery over your thoughts and feelings. Such mastery opens the door to freedom, joy and power undreamt of by the fear-stricken persona. In fact, making the state of gratitude your emotional headquarters will go a long way towards the subjugation of the persona into its rightful position of service to your Divine nature, whereby this mind and body become the instruments of expression for the Divine Presence within rather than the site of suffering, confusion and alienation.

Constantly inhabiting the state of gratitude will bring you into the greater appreciation of the profound beauty that surrounds us. You will find love flowering in your heart without effort and you will awaken with time to the truth of your eternal and Divine identity. Cultivating the grateful heart, making gratitude your emotional headquarters, must be the most beautiful and swiftly transcendent of all the faculties, capacities and gifts discussed in this book thus far. You will very soon see and feel the transformation of your interior world and this will, by the workings of the infallible law, begin to be expressed in your outer world also. The beauty flowering in your heart will meet its likeness in your day-to-day reality. By identifying and giving thanks for the good in your life, yet more good will come to you. By identifying and giving thanks for what you want, your desires will be fulfilled. Make no mistake, it is your birthright to be creative, expansive and prosperous; all of these gifts are open to the grateful heart yet the greatest boon to be gained from this practice is the connection that is thus secured with the Divine Presence within. The beauty, peace and joy made apparent with this drawing close to the Truth within is sublime and immutable. This wonder cannot be captured in words; you can only experience it to know it. It is worthy above all else of your sincere devotion because this drawing near to your true Divine nature is why you are here; it is the most profound purpose of your life and it is your path to liberation.

Cultivating the grateful heart could not possibly be more rewarding or more beautiful, but I invite you not to depend on my word. I invite you instead to do this for yourself; with an open mind and a sincere approach, cultivate a grateful heart and you will gather all the proof you could ever need of what I have suggested here. You will come to agree that it is not possible to do justice to the power of this practice with mere words. This single practice opens the way for you to gain the mastery of your own thoughts and emotions that will empower you to realise the fulfilment of your cherished dreams. Furthermore, this practice will simultaneously bring you into ever-closer accord with that Presence which is the source of your existence. There could be no greater recommendation to be made for anything that we could choose to do with our time and efforts whilst making our sojourn here.

Chapter Nine: Care

You must care

In the period leading up to the complete collapse of my health and the flight of all energy from my body, I lived in such a fashion that I showed no care for myself. I drove myself forward trying to secure stability for my family with little regard for my own well-being. This approach very nearly cost me my life. We are matter and if you want to behave as if you do not matter, then you may well reach the point where you cease to exist as matter. You do matter and you must care. You must care for yourself. You must love yourself regardless of what the world may have suggested to the contrary. When we fail to love and care for ourselves, we will lessen our capacity to care for and love others. I could do nothing more for my family when all energy had left my body and I lay under the weight of total exhaustion for what seemed like an eternity.

My quest for understanding and healing led me to look closely at my own life for the roots of my own ultimately self-destructive behaviour and I had to acknowledge that I was indeed playing out a pattern of behaviour that was established during my childhood. Even as a child, it was my role to look after everyone, even my parents (who were often to be found in various states of disrepair), but for all my efforts there was no thanks, only harsh words and physical abuse. As an adult, I came to understand the overwhelming nature of the pressures my parents were facing and were unable to transcend at that time in their lives. The feelings that arose from such experiences impressed my subconscious with the belief that I was not important and led to me constantly putting everyone's welfare before my own, and this behaviour persisted even into adulthood.

It was the awakening of the Divine Presence in me that helped me to overcome the shyness, anxiety and mistrust that my childhood experiences had engendered in me. Coming to understand the distinction between our persona and our true eternal and Divine nature is the key to healing and transcendence. In my case, I now understand that it was the persona that persecuted me as a child and it was the persona that felt so hurt and diminished. The Divine Presence was witness to all these dramas but remained untouched and untainted by any of them. I realized that the persona was to the fore in my family members who gave me such a rugged time, as well as the children, parents and teachers who were so hostile and bigoted at my school and that it was my persona that soaked up all the pain that was coming my way. It is easier to forgive and heal on the basis of this understanding. It is equally essential to heal the child who impressed the subconscious realm with so many negative feelings, feelings that would eventually create powerful patterns of behaviour that would undermine my future success and happiness. To begin to care for yourself is to begin to address these roots of suffering in your life.

Awareness is forever your starting point. Ask the silent witness of each and every event in your life to show you the roots of the behaviours that are sabotaging your success and happiness in life and you will be shown, sometimes in dreams, sometimes in waking visions, what happened in your formative years to create the patterns of thought, feeling and belief that are proving to be counterproductive for you now. Then, forgive all involved and tell the child the truth about its Divine identity. Let the child know that it was never the victim it was made to feel that it was, but rather, that it was always the Divine child of the Divine Presence that heals every wound and restores every broken heart.

You must care; you must do this because it clears the way for you to gain mastery over all the faculties discussed in this book and thus enable you to live up to the true and profound purpose of your life.

Care nurtures all the faculties

To care enough to make it your duty to understand what has been happening in your life, and why you are really here, is the beginning of salvation. Such care can open the door to the understanding that will set you free and give you mastery over your own thoughts and feelings. This mind, this body is the vehicle that will take us through this life. Without an understanding of the Divine nature that is fleetingly clothed with this vehicle of flesh and bone, we live under a fundamental miscomprehension of what our life is really about. We may succeed in many ways on the highway of life, but we will never fulfil the amazing potential of the vehicle in our possession if we remain ignorant of the power that is its source. To fulfil our potential here is to reflect the beauty, love and power that is our true nature.

Your ability to forgive yourself and others, your power to choose, the power of belief, your imagination, your capacity to feel positive emotions that will foster your well-being and prosperity, and your ability to nurture and sustain the grateful heart are all nourished by your capacity to care. Give each of these faculties your love and care and you will discover yourself able to more fully express your true nature. To turn your attention lovingly towards these gifts is to move towards the fullness of life. It is the Divine purpose for you to live more abundantly, meaning that you should enjoy life's riches to the utmost, whilst encouraging and empowering all who are interested to do the same. Generosity is your Divine nature, therefore, willingly give every good thing, in good measure, to all who are willing to receive, and just as importantly, be willing to receive all the good this wondrous life has to offer you. The attention you give every faculty discussed in this book should be characterised by love and care. Give all of these gifts the greatest care and they will reward your attention beyond measure. Let love and care meet with all your practices; let this become your means of engaging with life. Give each task, give each moment, give each thought, each feeling, each action your unstinting love and care. You will only be reflecting the truth of how precious your life is, how special and beautiful each moment, each breath is. To live like this is to acknowledge the sacred nature of your existence and to continuously pay homage with your attention, your love and your care. You will find yourself in love with life and everything within yourself that you give such love and care to will grow, flower and bear fruit in the most marvellous ways.

Altered states: a vehicle for healing

The work of developing and attaining mastery of the faculties highlighted in this book requires the appropriate healing of the damage done by a lifetime of negative and limiting impressions being made on the subconscious mind. Forgiveness has an important role to play in any healing formula since forgiveness acts to clear and cleanse the mind and heart of negativity, thus allowing easier access to the higher frequencies of the energy that will help to liberate your spirit.

The crux of the problem facing us is ever the same; it is our identity crisis that is at the root of all our suffering. We honestly believe that we are this body and mind, that we are this persona. From this illusory perspective arises all our difficulties here, all our fear and anxiety, every element in our sense of alienation stems from this fundamental misunderstanding of our own true nature. Any attempt to heal the dis-ease, disharmony or maladjustment that we feel here and experience as ill-health on all levels of our being, must address this fundamental issue in order to bring healing that will be complete and lasting. To be made whole we must awaken to our true identity.

We have a means of escaping the hold the persona exercises on our attention. In order to reach the subconscious where healing needs to take effect, altered states of consciousness have a valuable role to play. The states I speak of here are embodied in one word, 'relaxation'. The simple act of bringing deep relaxation to body and mind places us in easier touch with the subconscious whereby we can both give and receive vital information in regards to our healing and the central question of our true identity. Relax your body and mind whilst remaining alert and aware and you will experience a shift in consciousness that opens the way for healing and the development of your connection to your own Divine nature. Adopting the daily practice of entering the state of deep relaxation will facilitate the reshaping of your interior world. You will more easily become aware of the stillness, silence and peace that are at the source of your being. From this state of deep but highly aware repose, this place of profound stillness, all-pervading silence and peace, you recognise your true and Divine nature, you realise that you are Awareness itself, the Presence that is the One Witness of all things. Having verified your true identity, affirm the healing of your mortal body, affirm also the fulfilment of your heartfelt desires. Your desires for your good and that of others are gifts that will assist your expansion into the state of full realisation that you and the Source are one, both dreamer and dream inseparable and Divine.

During a period of my illness when I was too weak to read or write, I retreated to the stillness I had discovered deep within my own being. In that stillness, inspiration flowed into my mind and all I could do was record the words coming to me using a Dictaphone. The following is one such inspiration, a meditation that takes you into the altered state that enables you to recall your true nature:

Now, whether sitting or lying down, just begin to make yourself completely comfortable in whichever way is best for you. Now, gently become aware that you are breathing. Just notice that you are breathing. Notice the gentle in and out flow of the breath, then bring your awareness to your body. Become aware of the fact that there is a body and begin to relax, just begin to relax. Now, take your awareness to the top of your head and allow the whole of your head area to be filled with feelings and sensations of stillness, calmness and peace. Gently allow these feelings to roll down through your body, rolling down through your face, your neck, your shoulders and arms, hands and fingers, completely relaxed, relaxation rolling down through the chest, back, the abdomen, the thighs, the calves and shins, the feet, the bottom of the feet and the toes. The whole body is completely relaxed. Just become aware of this feeling of relaxation and the feeling of letting go of all tension in the body and mind.

Just become aware of this presence of stillness, calmness and peace. Notice how changeless it is, how constant it is. And all we need to do to realise this is simply to be aware of this changeless, peace-filled, calm Presence which is here. Once we begin to do this, we begin to realise that all changes are taking place within and are contained by the changeless. If you step back, you will be able to observe this. Feel the deep, spacious and calm peace of this fathomless Awareness. This is who we are. This is the great storehouse of health, strength, vitality, wealth and creativity, All-Knowing, All-Seeing Omnipresence. This is who we are. Become aware that there is a presence which is also aware of the observer. A still, silent, unchanging calmness, a presence of Supreme Peace. This sense of Peace; become aware of this only and stay with this. Let go of the urge to change anything, to understand anything, to do or undo anything. Just let all be as it is and stay with this Presence. Just feel yourself becoming more and more aware of this, because it is right here, right now. We don't need to do anything; we don't need to go anywhere. We don't need to go left or right, up or down, backward or forward. We just need to be aware and feel and know that nothing else is required, as this is our essential Self. This is the real us, this is who we are. So, remember your first Self and be at ease here and now.

Feel the healing presence of the Self. Everything is contained here and is within this. Our true Self is total, changeless, inexhaustible. It has no beginning; it has no end. It is constant, it is the only thing that is constant; it is the Source of everything we can perceive and all that we cannot perceive. So, become aware of this still, calm, spacious, warm Presence, which contains everything, yet, at the same time, remains still and unchanged. It is not affected by our emotions, our thoughts, seeing, hearing, feeling; it remains the same whilst all these things and activities are taking place; it remains changeless, calm, still and peace-filled. Be aware of this, drift deeper into this Self, stay with this, as this is who we are. We can't know this Self intellectually, we can only be it, so just be at ease with your Self. Be still, be calm, be silent, let go of thoughts, let go of worries, let go of memories, let go of emotions, let go of feelings, let go of planning or plotting, just let go of all these things. Just be at ease with whatever is and stay with the Self. Notice the observer, observing these things, these actions, these activities and just move behind the observer and stay as the Pure Presence of Awareness. Stay with Awareness, staying with the pure, untouched, changeless, calm, healing, peace-filled Awareness. Remain in this state for at least ten minutes. This is the end of this meditation called 'Be your Self'.

It may help for you to record this meditation and play it back to yourself.

Deliberately assuming the state of deep relaxation and proceeding as described above on a regular basis will begin to shape your mundane experiences in a remarkable way. Genuine progress made on the inner planes must, in due course, be reflected in your outer world. Inhabiting the altered state of awareness marked by such deep relaxation is an important element of the care we owe our own spirit on this amazing sojourn we call life.

The moments that bridge wakefulness and sleep also offer a portal of access to the subconscious realm that should not be ignored. Guard what you ferry over that bridge into sleep. Be deliberate in ordering your thoughts just before the descent into sleep. Scorn negativity; leave negative, limiting thoughts and emotions alone in favour of your visions of your wishes fulfilled, accompanied by the appropriately profound feelings of joy and gratitude that would accompany the fulfilment of your dreams. See and feel your healing, your prosperity, your happiness, your spiritual liberation as accomplished facts and the subconscious realm will be bound by the infallible law to create (within the fullness of time) their likeness in your waking reality. How you approach the hours of sleep represents another important and powerful element of the care you provide for yourself whilst here. Knowingly utilise the altered state experienced in the moments just before slumber to your great advantage rather than allowing your anger, regret, anxiety or loathing to accompany you there and thus poison the subconscious realm and create further suffering for you in the future. Be certain not to underestimate the significance of the emotional state you adorn yourself with as you fall asleep. Approach sleep with the deep sense of love and care I suggested above and you will be left with no doubt that our world is being shaped in the depths of our consciousness even as we sleep, seemingly unaware of a single thing.

Remembrance and resurrection

The illusion of being a persona is a state of forgetfulness, even dismemberment, which leaves you feeling separated and alienated in ways that often cannot be understood. The state of deep relaxation opens the way for this sense of alienation to be transcended and replaced with the realisation of your essential unity with Being itself. We are normally so entranced and enthralled with the outer world that we do not take time to be truly still, truly silent, truly at peace. The state of deep relaxation brings us to the realm that holds the secret of our true identity and our boundless potential. We are encouraged at every turn to exert ourselves and summon ever-greater efforts in order to achieve our objectives, but there is a world of power and clarity that is repulsed by effort and that is only accessed in the state of effortlessness. It is the retreat from the physical and mental exertions of the persona that permits the beginning of remembrance. In stillness, in effortlessness, our identity can be reassembled, we can be healed and the breath of new life can be breathed into us.

The ancient stories of the perfected soul being murdered, dismembered and scattered in all directions, or in other variations being crucified, all have the common denominator of resurrection and an equally common esoteric meaning in that these stories speak of the potential for each and every one of us to remember our true nature and to rise from the seeming annihilation of our Divine nature to the full realisation of our immortal and pristine Self. The stories which speak of the hero or saviour archetype speak of the saviour in each one of us which is none other than our own Divine nature. The saviour, the perfected soul is our own Awareness itself. The altered states I speak of here allow this realisation to grow in power and significance until no doubt remains and our resurrection is complete. At this point, even the persona will bow and acknowledge the Saviour's right to rule in your life and to exercise sovereignty over your subconscious realm. Such remembrance and resurrection would represent liberation from suffering and deliverance into heaven here on earth, since heaven is merely the appellation for the supreme state of consciousness embodied by our unity with our own Divine nature, Awareness itself.

The role of discipline

Even in the midst of our individual and collective horror stories, I know there exists the eternal hope that we can transform our circumstances and somehow satisfy our indomitable desire for love, joy, peace and prosperity. The persona fearfully tries to outwit the workings of fate, the machinations of other personas and the limitations arising from its own deluded nature in its efforts to fulfil our most enduring desires. But failure stalks such fear-driven attempts at fulfilment because, even when the persona triumphantly achieves an objective, it is not long before the haunting voice of dissatisfaction and discontent is heard mocking your achievements. Some personas have fear pitched so high that all efforts at success are destroyed even before they begin. Stagnation will be a loyal companion in such cases. We are told that if we apply discipline, we cannot fail; success must follow discipline and hard work.

True success is the realisation of the desire that lies beneath each and every desire we will ever have, the fulfilment of which will bring us complete satisfaction and bliss, and this is the desire to be reunited with our true, original and Divine nature. Each and every desire, no matter how seemingly insignificant or diverse, is leading us home to this one imperishable goal. When we achieve this goal, all others are effortlessly within our command. Will discipline bring us victory in our quest for Self-Realisation?

I have advocated constancy in regard to the practices that would bring mastery over your thoughts and emotions and I have suggested constancy is required to cultivate the grateful heart. Even if you wish to become physically fit, constancy in taking the appropriate exercise is required. I'm sure most people would agree that it requires discipline to develop the constancy that will bring you success. However, we would not suggest that it requires discipline to brush our teeth on a daily basis because brushing our teeth has become a habit, something we do effortlessly without hesitation. Our habits create our way of life and our way of life brings us the results we see in health, wealth, happiness and the nature of our relationships. If we can establish the practices described above as our habit, as our way of life, we will feel no need to speak of discipline or onerous effort. The mastery of the beautiful faculties discussed in this book involves practices that are so pleasurable to undertake and so rewarding that they should all be approached in the spirit of love and gratitude. Make constancy in developing these faculties your way of life and your life will reveal the wonder, power and beauty that sustains our existence. In due course, your own experiences will confirm the astonishing truth of who you really are.

Care and attention

Caring to understand the true purpose of your life will lead you to give your attention to the question of your true identity and the faculties discussed throughout this book, because, these things reveal your profound purpose for being here. You automatically give your attention to that which you care about most. There are, however, powerful interests calling your attention away from that which would bring your highest good, in favour of that which they perceive will enrich and empower them rather than you.

Since you can make no progress towards your awakening without directing your attention in the right way, it becomes crucial that you use your power to choose to transcend the multitude of competing distractions that would deny you that priceless treasure. These distractions assail you on a daily basis but you do have the means to turn your back on them in favour of your desire for the happiness and freedom which is your innermost reality.

Start by taking inventory of what you are giving your attention to. What dominates your attention currently? And does the destiny of your own soul get a look in? Take a typical day in your life and make an honest appraisal of where your attention goes during such a day. You may learn a great deal about why you feel the way you do and why you are experiencing the things you are experiencing in your life. How much of your attention is going towards what you truly care about? Is what you truly care about favourable to your well-being? The answers to these questions will help you to make the choices that may need to be made in order to do justice to the power of care and attention in your life. If your attention is dominated by the machinations of your persona, or that of another's persona, or that of the personas being highlighted in the media, then you may notice the negativity such attention fosters. You may also notice that the goals achieved through such attention are hard-won and that the satisfaction gained, thus, is short-lived, soon to be replaced by another fear-driven request from the persona.

The call for your care and attention ultimately comes from the persona, which cannot survive without your attention, or from your true Divine nature, without which you cannot live the fullness of life. Everything in the world competing for your attention can be reduced to this distinction between the persona and the Self. In each moment, we make our choice. So, having taken our inventory, we can ask ourselves in each moment who claims my attention, the persona or the Divine Presence?

Your care changes the universe

Attending with love and with care to each moment, to each choice, will not only empower you to enjoy the fullness of life here and now but you will find yourself face to face with fundamental mysteries surrounding the nature of our existence. Experiencing your unity with Awareness itself brings you to a place of awe and complete liberation. This Presence in you holds the entire universe in its embrace and is one with every created thing, including your body and mind, so that it dawns on you that you are not a speck in the universe, but rather, the universe is taking place in you. Without your existence, there is no universe. Without Awareness, there can be no consciousness., Without the dreamer, there can be no dream.

Now you realise that you have a relationship to the entire universe, the nature of which you could never have anticipated. Your imagination has no limit save that which you place on it yourself. This is also true of your Will and your power of belief. Once you accept that you are not just your body, you begin to appreciate the limitless potential afforded you by the subtle dimensions of your being.

You can thus begin to know that you are not just the helpless victim of your circumstances, but rather, that your true nature is one with Divine Intelligence and is able to transform any situation without the stress, toil and anxiety characteristic of the persona's attempts to manipulate its world.

The development and mastery of the faculties discussed here will provide you with proof of your truly boundless nature. Once you begin to sense your unity with Divine Intelligence and you start to understand that these faculties are merely the means for this Divine Intelligence to have full expression (through you) on this plane of existence, you will be left in no doubt that you are far more than you could ever have imagined previously. You will recognise your persona's very limited perspective of your humanity as illusory and you will find yourself in a very exalted state of awe regarding the truth that has been hidden beyond that illusion for so long.

In reaching such a point, care must be taken to balance the exalted, blissful sense of Self-realisation with the groundedness that will enable you to fully participate in the manifestation of life on the earthly plane. Realising the truth about your own Divine nature need not lead to you 'dropping out' or becoming a recluse. Without doubt, you need periods of serious retreat where you enjoy true solitude in order to strengthen your union with the Self, however, the truth should set you free to live in an authentic way wherever you are and to make your own unique contribution to the affairs of the world. You can live fearlessly, making your addition to the greater good; you can live passionately whilst, all the time, being sublimely detached, since your peace cannot be disturbed by the world drama.

Participate fully in the world but from the place of Supreme Peace and you would have honoured the profound reason for your presence here.

Life

I am now a mature woman, so I have lived long enough to have asked myself what this life is all about. I have suffered terrible experiences throughout my life since my earliest childhood, enough to make me wonder if life was some sort of sadistic practical joke on behalf of some fiendish entity that gathered pleasure from the torture of the human soul. An atheist comes to mind, insisting that there is no God, and that if such a deity does exist, 'he' must be a sadist for allowing the tumult of suffering that exists in the world.

Despite all my own personal pain and suffering and the horrors I have seen taking place around me during my life, I have never doubted the existence of a Supreme Being and I have never doubted the beneficence of that Being. Even as a child, I felt the presence of Beneficence in the midst of everything, although, I could not relate the divinity I felt aware of, to the man in the sky I was taught about at school and in my mother's church. That Presence is the Indomitable Spirit after which this book is named and by the Grace of that Divine Presence, I have come to know the wonderful truth about my life that would make all the torment I've suffered and seen pale and insignificant by comparison.

Awakening to the fact that the Supreme Being is not a distant patriarch but dwells within me, within us all, closer than our very breath, revolutionised my understanding of life and enabled me to fearlessly face every challenge that life could present me with thereafter. The peace found in this Presence is unbreakable and acts as a great liberation from the turmoil created by my persona or that of anyone else. This peace is the root of the tree and the faculties spoken of above are the branches which will bear the fruits that our mastery of self will produce.

This understanding has marked the arrival of miracles in my own life; miracles of healing and miracles of victory against powerful and unjust adversaries, and it can do the same for you. The Divine Presence can never fail you; all that is required is your sincere attention. No matter the grave or fearful nature of the problems facing you, I promise you that if you sincerely turn to the Divine Intelligence and surrender all your doubts and fears, you will be amazed at the course of events that will set you free from the grasp of your tribulations. The Indomitable Spirit within you will guide you in the use of the faculties which will bring you victory, transcendence and the true riches of life, even in situations which may appear to be impossible. Your life is the means for this Spirit to find full expression in the realm of time and space, this is how truly remarkable your life is. Never again allow any person or event to persuade you otherwise. Cherish, honour and adore your life and the great Spirit within you that waits silently to lift you above the confines of your persona's illusory worldview.

Chapter Ten:
Divine Love

Love affairs of the human heart

Anyone who has experienced the feeling of being in love will attest to the joy and the beauty that such a feeling can bring into your life. Finding yourself in love with another introduces you to a new and wondrous dimension of life. Mundane events are enlivened and the world appears to be brighter in every way due to the elevated feelings in your own heart. Just the sight of the one you love could make you tingle all over. Why then does being in love so often end up as a heart-breaking experience? Once again, the dichotomy between our persona and our true nature is at play here. We see in another a reflection of our own Divine nature which ignites the recognition of that nature within us, thus we get a glimpse of the bliss that we really are.

The problem arises when we mistakenly begin to believe that the other person is now responsible for sustaining our joy. The persona's fear-driven, insecure and selfish world-view can very quickly begin to sabotage the heavenly feelings you had every right to wish for from this being in love. The flaws apparent in the one you love are the fruits of the persona; so too is your dependency on that person to sustain the wonderful feeling that being in love first brought you. This is how the persona can transform the love affairs of the human heart into nightmarish dramas.

It is not surprising then that many souls become sceptical, even cynical about love, feeling that the whole thing is some sort of terrible trick. Such beliefs will, of course, bear faithful fruit in your experience if they have been impressed upon your subconscious mind with sufficient force. This is a sad reality since we would miss altogether the powerful message the experience of being in love is always bringing us. Even if our relationship fails (i.e., we are unable to transcend the work being done by the persona to subvert the reign of love in our lives), we should never deny the truth behind the glory of being in love. Regardless of how you may have been brought down to earth from that elevated state, the joy you felt in that state was real and was an indication of your true and original state of being. Whatever the persona does to obscure the truth and sustain its hold on your life, it can never diminish the power and the beauty of the peace and love that is your innermost reality. The sincere love you feel for your lover, husband, wife, relations, friends, etc., is an expression of your true nature. The world that the persona has established acts in so many ways to thwart the reign of love in our lives, however, the more you are able to free yourself from the grip of your own persona, the more the reality of love's power will bloom in your life.

All cynicism regarding love will shrivel and turn to dust when you realise that the love affairs of the human heart are just a fleeting shadow of the true glory of our Divine nature. Even physical love, the act of physical union with another soul, can bring us a sense of transcendence and bliss since union is the essence of love. The feeling of being one with another, one with creation itself, is itself a state of bliss. Thus, love affairs of the human heart give us clues to a state that has fathomless dimensions of beauty which can lift us up above the turmoil and pain that often surrounds the persona's interpretation of love.

The depths of Unity

Our identification with our body and mind convinces us of our individuality and our separateness from everyone and everything else. We are, however, absolutely one with existence. Our being is inseparable from existence itself and this is true of every soul; we are all present in the Unity underlying all existence. To become aware of this truth, to experience our intrinsic unity with everything is to experience an indescribable sense of bliss and complete satisfaction. This is the root of our longing for love and the drive to escape our sense of alienation. If we are able to loosen the hold the persona has on our consciousness and abide in our true nature, we will increasingly become aware of the Unity which we truly are. The depth of this Unity is limitless and is the essence of the Divine Love which is the womb and the mother of all things. Our journey into the depths of Unity is our journey into the depths of joy. This awakening from the dream of separation from the Source marks the emergence of healing, healing which addresses all the injury and pain the illusion of separation has caused us. This Unity, this Divine Love meets every need, since nothing at all stands outside it. It is Intelligence itself, which understands every problem and every solution in faultless detail. Moving into the depths of Unity, there is no failure; only the persona has failed us and, even then, each failure was a call for your soul to come home to this Unity, a call to return to the depths of Divine Love.

Matchless Beauty

Our existence is truly amazing. If we can take the time to deeply contemplate the nature of our existence, the mystery of being itself, you cannot fail to begin to feel awe for the miracle of being alive and being aware. Such contemplation will open the door to a growing appreciation of the beauty involved in the adventure of living. Beauty is one of life's greatest riches and it surrounds us all on every side. We live on an amazingly beautiful planet. The natural world is full of awe-inspiring beauty, hence, a walk in natural surroundings can transform your mood, lifting you above your burdens by virtue of the profound effect natural beauty can have on us.

Human creativity can also produce objects of soul-stirring beauty. We can find music, film, literature, painting, art of all types of such beauty that transports us beyond the normal passage of time into a state of deep appreciation for the wonder of being alive. Beauty is a source of profound joy to the human soul. If our lives were bereft of beauty, we would descend into a state of numb indifference. How could the human spirit soar in the absence of beauty? And yet, it is possible to find ourselves estranged from all the wondrous beauty in this world according to our own state of mind at any given time. If our mind is beset with the negativity that the persona can so often produce, we could comprehensively miss the majesty and splendour that life has blessed us all with. But if we are able to transcend the mental shackles created by the persona and begin to look at our world through grateful eyes, we will not fail to discover the beauty that has been hidden in plain view all around us.

When I turn my thoughts to the part beauty has played in rescuing me from the most trying passages in my own life, my memory of the beauty found in a group of people surrendered to Love remains unequalled. Many years ago, during my late teens, I had the great privilege to be befriended by a group of people (the likes of which I have never met again) who had dedicated themselves to the love of Love itself. I found these men and women to be a great inspiration. Their kindness, grace and purity of spirit were the most beautiful things I could have wished to experience at that time in my life.

These people were radiant. The brightness of spirit emanating from them was physically apparent and this proved to me early in my life how amazingly beautiful the human spirit can be, once wedded to the power of Love. To be in the company of these souls was such a wonderful experience; the atmosphere surrounding them was so uplifting and enlivening. Feeling the togetherness and unity nurtured by the Love that these exceptional friends embodied left an impression with me that has never faded. Sadly for me, these friends left the country and I eventually lost contact with them due to the turmoil overwhelming their homeland at that time, but they will forever hold a special place in my memory because they introduced me to the unassailable beauty which is the garden formed by Love once it is allowed true expression in the human heart.

My friends did not nurture this extraordinary beauty in themselves in a haphazard way. They arrived at their majestic state by way of deliberate attention and by following a particular way of life. They were a marvellous example to me (as such a young person then) of what was possible when you put Love at the pinnacle of your consciousness. I have not experienced anything more beautiful than witnessing the love and unity exemplified by these humble yet extraordinary people.

Grace has allowed me to come to know, beyond doubt, that the source of the matchless beauty I experienced those many years ago remains changeless and unchallenged. Only the persona stands in the way of us remembering this most precious facet of the Divine Presence. This Love brings a mysterious luminosity to your countenance. It awakens the awareness of the beauty within and thus ushers beauty into all your paths. Following the complete collapse of my health and the subsequent revival of the (by then dormant) recognition of my interior world, I came to understand the glory of the energy I had seen so well-expressed in those aforementioned friends. This exalted state has brought me joy that cannot be described, in the midst of turmoil and disturbances that would otherwise have left me in despair. Now, I know for myself the supremacy of Love over all the fleeting phenomena of life. No matter what had risen up to challenge my peace of mind, the mere contemplation of the unchanging beauty of this Love has set me free and delivered me victory over every test. The purity of this Love is the key to its invincibility; it is also the key to the total security of the soul in its embrace.

The persona has brought so much ugliness into the world with its fear-driven perspective on life. Looking deeply at my own life, I can attest to the ugliness that my persona has created due to the negative conditioning it has received and absorbed since childhood. Not until I began to understand the workings of the subconscious mind did I start to appreciate the importance of the beauty I had found within my own heart and its power to cleanse my subconscious of the negative and limiting beliefs that would subvert my good.

All those years ago, I had noticed the atmosphere of auspiciousness that enveloped those friends whose very presence revealed a priceless secret. Grace was with them. I also know that their practice of constantly giving their attention to Love worked to cleanse the subconscious realm in such a manner as to empower all the faculties of the spirit. I have seen, time and time again, with my own eyes, the manifestation of goals that appeared to be practically impossible or the emergence of situations that could only be described as the result of Divine intervention. If you seek this beauty in your own nature, you will validate the things described here for yourself, by way of your own personal experience. There can be nothing more beautiful to know than this precious Love hidden within the innermost depths of your own heart.

Love and the Law of Vibration

The universe is governed by certain laws which operate and dictate the shape and form of our experiences here, whether we are aware of these laws or not. It is far better for us to be aware of, and to understand these laws that represent the framework within which our lives take place. This would be the worthy subject of another book altogether, but, for the sake of our purposes here, it is important to consider the law of vibration. This relates to the fact that everything in creation has a vibration; everything is moving at a particular rate. Even a stone is vibrating at a given rate even though this movement will not be perceptible to the human eye, at the molecular level, even a stone is vibrating. Everything has a vibration. From gross, solid things like stones all the way through to subtle, invisible things like our thoughts and emotions, everything has a vibration. It is also important to note that, in terms of vibrations at the level of the subtle realms, like attracts like. The stronger the vibration, the stronger the attractive force. This is why the nature and the force of your thoughts and emotions are so critical. Your thoughts and emotions have vibrations which can create magnetism for good or ill.

Fear, hate, jealousy and envy have vibrations that create destruction, pain and suffering. Love has a vibration that brings healing, joy and beauty into the world. We have the power to attract the good our hearts desire by the wise use of the law of vibration. Love engenders life's most wonderful bounty; harmony, balance, unity, justice, peace, happiness, prosperity, creativity, warmth, compassion, forgiveness, redemption, courage and freedom. It opens the storehouse of life's blessings. It is foremost amongst all the positive vibrations you could wish to indulge and sustain in your own mind. The riches you invite into your life by holding the vibration of Love are limitless. It will lift you into the realms of life's deepest mystery whilst grounding you here in the midst of the mundane challenges of day-to-day living.

The vibration of Love holds immense power, a power far greater than the vibrations of the fear or the greed or the hate that have seduced the persona and covered the world in pain for so many ages. The power of Love is unassailable; nevertheless, pure Love has been mostly ignored by humanity in favour of the lower vibrations which have created so much havoc for us, individually and collectively. The only reason the truly awesome power of Love is not self-evident to the vast majority of people is that there are so few people who have sincerely surrendered to that power and allowed that vibration to flow perpetually through their hearts to take effect in their lives.

The persona has little faith that it could survive without struggling to manipulate people and situations to accomplish its fear-driven objectives. It cannot imagine a life driven by Love rather than fear. When genuine Love makes an appearance in our lives, the persona tends to want to contaminate our experience with its payload of fear, jealousy, insecurity, selfishness, possessiveness, envy, pride and yet more fear; weeds enough to ruin the beautiful garden of Love, if they are left to grow.

Pure Love, uncontaminated by the persona's fear etc., is our original and true nature; this is why our souls long for Love. We long to return to the state of bliss that gave birth to existence. This is a profound mystery, yet it is accessible to us all. When we use our power of choice to choose the Self over the persona, we unlock the code to the vibration of Love in our own being. Only then do we begin to get an inkling of who we truly are. We begin to experience our unity with the whole creation. This is a feeling which is impossible to describe beyond suggesting a state of complete satisfaction and peace.

There is also the sense of meeting the unconditioned Love at the root of all things. Thus, we begin to recognise the vibration of the greatest power in existence. It sustains us all; even as we choose fear and greed and hate instead of Love, it is Love that gives us our immortal being and allows us to dream that we are other than Love. To what end? I feel our epic journey in duality, feeling separate from our true nature, is just that, an epic journey of experience that allows the Self to know the Self anew. Having known fear and hate, Love comes to know itself anew.

Gaining mastery over your own thoughts and feelings is the key to being able to align yourself with the vibration of Love. Whilst on the road to such mastery, the company you keep becomes very important. It will help greatly to minimise the time spent in the company of those who are hostile, hateful, false and ill-meaning, as such vibrations will not encourage your progress. It is challenging enough to put your own persona in its rightful place of subservience to your Divine nature without struggling with other people who are stuck in the egoic mind.

Seek out company which reflects that which you seek. Become sensitive to the vibration surrounding people and places. What you feel is more significant than what you see or hear in most cases. The persona can become very skilled at presenting an attractive facade behind which it can conceal its nefarious agendas. Pay attention to what you feel in order to discern the vibrations around you. On developing true mastery over your own thoughts and emotions, you will have the power to rise above any negative vibrations that arise in your experience, but, until then, it will pay you to avoid the company of those who would affect your thoughts and emotions (and therefore your vibrations) in a negative way. Change your dominant emotional state and see what takes place in your life. The vibration of Love, Peace and gratitude, constantly present in your heart, will elevate you above all tribulations and introduce you to the fullness of life.

How then do you align yourself with the vibration of Love? Choose Love. Turn your thoughts to Her over and over again until this becomes your habitual pattern of thought. Contemplate Her nature deeply. Delve into this realm with all your heart and soul. Be in love with Love. You have heard of lovers saying they think of their beloved all the time, that their beloved is never out of their thoughts; well, make Love itself your beloved and you will find yourself in love with your own true nature.

Call Her name constantly; just keep repeating silently in your own mind Love, Love, Love, incessantly Love and imbibe the beautiful atmosphere accompanying this invocation. Feel this energy embracing your consciousness. Make this invocation constantly and feel Love's reply emerging in your own presence. Make each call heartfelt, because you are calling Love to take over your whole existence. Make each call a complete surrender and it will be impossible for you not to become powerfully aware of the Divine Presence operating in your life.

In the moments of stillness when you are not making your invocation, in the silent depths of your own being, research Her nature. The atmosphere found there will become yours. You will be in harmony and perfect alignment with Love's vibration. The power revealed will be yours, as, in truth, it has always been throughout eternity.

The path of devotion

Being in love with Love opens the gates to a glorious kingdom hidden right here in our midst. Your sincerity is essential; it will inspire your devotion and your devotion will deepen your experience of Love. The lotus flowering in your heart will be revealed despite the murky waters of worldly experience. Your devotion will ignite the flames of constancy that will have you basking in Love's radiance. Deep contemplation of Love's nature and the calling of Love's name in the spirit of surrender and adoration are steps on the path of devotion but they are not alone. In time, you will begin to see Love's handiwork all around you, in the natural world and in the essence of your fellow beings, and seeing Love's mark on the world, your soul will celebrate.

Music plays a special role in nurturing the spirit of devotion. Beautiful love songs of all genres can bring you instant joy when they are interpreted as songs about the love of Love itself. Music touches our spirit directly, which is why it is such a powerful way to deepen our relationship with Love. The right kind of music very swiftly helps you to achieve harmony with the vibration of Love. The path of devotion is the road to a growing involvement with the vibration of Love, until we awaken to the Reality that we are the Love we seek.

At some of the most testing moments in my own life, songs that I regard as songs of devotion to the Divine Presence in us all, have immediately lifted me above the temptation to despair, into a state of complete joy. Beautiful love songs are such a strong trigger for the memory of the deeply sincere devotional feeling which throws you into Love's embrace. That embrace enables you to transcend the burden of your worldly woes.

Devotional music of many different genres sparks the devotional feeling in my own heart and this applies to secular love songs as well as formally religious devotional music, hymns, spirituals, bhajans etc. The sincerity as well as the giftedness of the singers and musicians provide the vehicle for this magical phenomenon to occur. An interviewer asked one of my favourite singers of secular love songs to explain why she did not seem to be ageing and she explained that thinking about and singing about love for all these years had kept her in a joyful and positive state of mind, and that, she believed, had contributed to her enduring youthfulness. For me, a profound mystery surrounds the power of devotional music (including secular love songs) to transport us to the sublime scenery of Love's domain. Our visits to this domain bring rewards which cannot be quantified but would indeed include the boon of a shining countenance and the youthfulness experienced by the aforementioned singer. Let music be your companion on the path of devotion and you will discover for yourself the nature of the riches found in her company.

Devotion suggests constancy and, in this case, constancy is not onerous or tiresome, requiring feats of willpower and iron discipline, since this path is so satisfying. Keeping Love's company is its own sweet reward. You will be well motivated to remain faithful to Love once you sincerely and unswervingly turn your attention to Her.

In each moment, you can keep company with Love and, in silence, deeply contemplate the mystery and power of Love, this Love that is the womb of creation. Beyond your contemplation of the inexhaustible glory of Love, fall back into silence and just feel the power of Love present throughout all existence and feel that same boundless power in your own heart. No-one need convince you of Love's power and glory when it is yours to experience in the realm of your own consciousness. This is the path, giving your attention, your thoughts, feelings and actions to Love and this path leads to freedom, joy and the most complete contentment. This path of devotion leads to the Truth that cannot fail to set you free. Love is that Truth, the unchanging Reality.

Seek the company of others who are in love with Love, the company of those who know this secret is precious. Time spent with the lovers of Love assists your progress on the path, especially when you are a sapling in Love's sacred grove. The company of other lovers of Love will nourish you in the most profound ways and deepen your understanding of Love's mystery. If you are blessed to meet other lovers of Love along your way, be deeply grateful and enjoy the miracle which such a meeting represents. In case you are yet to stumble across such rare souls as the lovers of Love truly are, do not be discouraged because nothing can stop you from keeping company with Love itself, within your own heart and this is sufficient to elevate you beyond everything that may hinder your full awakening to the Self.

The mystery at the source of Being

The true nature of Love is a profound mystery. Though this Love gives birth to us and sustains us, it is appreciated by the very few. The struggles of daily life obscure the magnificence of this Divine energy which is the essence of life itself. But those who can, by Grace, turn their attention towards Love, holding Love in their thoughts, in their feelings and in their actions, they will find life becoming a perpetual revelation. Beneficence, tenderness and power reveal themselves as Love's cosmic mystery unfurls within you, in the realm beyond words.

Awareness is silently present, hidden, immutable but rarely acknowledged, yet Divine Love is equally at one with us yet even more subtly hidden beyond the reach of the persona's world-view. The path of devotion leads you away from the clutches of the persona into the depths of Love's miracles. The womb of creation, our mother, Divine Love has gifts for us beyond our comprehension, but her enigma relents before our sincerity, devotion, humility and love.

At the Source of Being, Divine Love exists as formless, un-differentiated, holding the potential for everything. Our journey is a journey back to our Self; that which we are and have always been has become a profound mystery. When we are born into this realm of duality, it is as if we never ever knew of our true essence and we are trapped in a dream of conditions, not knowing that our true nature transcends all conditions. The drama of life is underpinned by our longing for happiness and freedom which is nothing beyond our longing to awaken from the dream of conditions, to arise in the light of Love which is our unconditioned, changeless and eternal nature.

Why would the Self journey in ignorance of itself? A journey filled with suffering and pain, with the answer everywhere present but veiled so effectively that so few discover it. Why? The perfection of the Self is eternal; we are eternal Bliss. You are, right now (regardless of all appearances), what you have always and will always be; Divine Love, Supreme Peace and Absolute Purity. By dreaming the world drama, you experience duality; you experience something other than perfection and bliss. Having forgotten your Self so completely, when you awaken from your dream of being the persona, you will appreciate the truth of who you are in a new, even more exalted way. Unity could only dream of separation and alienation in order to see its own glory in a new light. Now, having known fear, greed (the fear of lack) and hatred (the fear of others), Love understands its own glory all the more. This drama we call life on earth is a moment of self-exploration by the eternal Self.

The dream could not be more real for us earthlings but the means for us to awaken to the amazing and glorious truth of who we are exists here and now. Turn evermore from the dream to the dreamer; turn evermore to Love and the mystery will kindly share its secret with you. Your dream will be transformed, your pain and suffering will be healed, your own true nature will be redeemed and remembered in you and you will be resurrected from the deep sleep of the persona, to walk knowingly as the dreamer of this whole world drama, the emissary of Love on earth. You walk now with your feet firmly on the earth but you are free from fear, free from the delusions spun by the persona, you are filled with the joy that Love brings, you know now that you are what you have always been the Source and the essence of Being Itself, Supreme Love.

Love In Action

This wondrous Love is endlessly mysterious, but it is not just an abstract concept, it is a living force that finds expression in us, in our behaviour, in ways that powerfully shape our daily lives. Its presence can be felt in our aura; it has its own beautiful vibration and it becomes apparent in our actions. Love turns up as compassion. Having empathy for the plight of others and taking inspired action to alleviate or stop the suffering involved is the essence of compassion. This is one of the expressions of Love most redemptive to the human soul to both the givers and receivers of its gift. True compassion does not feed on the neediness of others. True compassion does not seek praise or recognition but is concerned with bringing genuine, effective help where it is needed. True compassion seeks to help those in need of help to get back to the place where they can help themselves, back to the place where they can know their own power. True compassion is a most beautiful expression of our Divine nature.

Love also shows up in our lives as Intelligence. This Intelligence knows and understands what the persona cannot know or understand. This intelligence is of a different order; being cognizant of every dimension involved in our experiences, it is able to bring inspiration that would make no sense to the logical mind. The unseen and unknown realms of existence that also have bearing on our lives are encompassed by this Intelligence. This extraordinary Intelligence works to bring the whole into balance and harmony. If we are tuned in to this order of intelligence and trust the inspiration it provides, we will be amazed at how things fall into place.

By contrast, the intelligence directed by the persona creates ever more ingenious ways to produce division, conflict, pain and destruction. The most brilliant minds in the scientific community have contributed to the creation of the most fiendish weapons ever made. Great intelligence devoid of wisdom becomes a very dangerous thing. The awakening of the intelligence directed by Love becomes a critical factor in shaping the future of humanity.

It is Love that acts to bring healing into our lives. It is the raw material for every healing process. Love purifies, restores, rejuvenates and vitalises any organism it is directed at, be that a sick body, a sick relationship, a sick organisation, a sick nation or a sick world. The world's imprisonment by the persona is the only reason this simple truth is not commonly known and experienced.

This healing power brings redemption even to those who would appear to be beyond redemption. The despairing, broken-hearted, defeated soul is not beyond the redemptive power of Love. The down-cast and the outcast are not beyond the reach of Love's power. If you give up on all else, never give up on Love. It will act through others to redeem you and it can act through you to redeem others. Never doubt its power to lift us up out of the deepest abyss into its magnificent light.

You need not believe in someone who has lost all belief in themselves or the validity of their life. You need not believe in your ability to motivate such a person to change, you need only believe in Love's boundless power in order to act as an instrument of redemption in such a person's life.

We act as a conduit of Love's power when we sacrifice some valued thing in order to protect or help another. Love can express itself in you as selfless action; underlying such action is the recognition of our essential unity. Sacrifice can be the greatest expression of love humanly possible. Some have sacrificed their own lives for those they love. The limitless mystery at the heart of Love lifts any sacrifice, no matter how great, above the realms of burden into the realms of immeasurable blessing. The sacrifice fuelled by love acts to open the portal to transcendence for both those making such sacrifice and those receiving the protection or help provided by such acts.

Commitment, too, flows from this sacred source. What motivates true devotion, loyalty and dedication aside from Love? Fuelled by love, you will be steadfast in your commitment to the beloved. In such a materialist age, it is common to see how quickly and easily the bonds of love are broken by sickness or financial reverses. Love would not abandon you in your hour of need; no, it would endure and seek the means to make things better. And it does have the means to make even seemingly impossible situations bow in its Light.

The source of uncommon courage, it will bring you the strength and bravery required when the roaring lions of trials and tribulations beset you. Knowing Love to be your true nature, you will appreciate the fearlessness which fills your heart as you look on serenely at the fear-stricken ideas of the persona when facing life's most dire challenges.

The Divine Presence within you is the source of the strength, inspiration and bravery required to work for justice in a world piled high with the injustices created by the persona/egoic mind. True seekers after freedom know that the awakening of the soul to its true identity is the greatest prerequisite for the growth of justice and freedom on this planet. Again, the lack of such an awakening could lead to our planet becoming, by degrees, a technologically controlled prison of the human soul. In each moment, we have the means to be free, to be fearless, simply by being still and silent enough to begin to discern our true and essential identity, which is Love itself. The courage demanded by the perilous age we inhabit is found within us where our true nature resides. This innate courage is equal to every kind of challenge; moral, intellectual or physical. Allied with the Divine intelligence which directs our actions with wisdom, this courage will bring you victory over all the perversities of the persona, whether they arise within you or in the outer world.

The surrender to Love also brings patience to bear on your relationship with life. Fortitude and serenity beyond the scope of the persona is the gift of your Divine nature. Such a gift will enable you to prevail over seemingly insurmountable circumstances. The power of patience to carry you to the accomplishment of the most daunting objectives cannot be overestimated. Many would have gained the prize if only they had possessed the patience to endure a little more. Your true Self will never fail to give you the patience you need to triumph over every challenge. Neither will you be left lacking the patience required to fully rediscover your authentic character. You must be able to serenely watch the persona trying to sustain its hold on your consciousness even after you have awoken to the amazing truth of your divine identity and the bliss this awakening represents. The persona is not real and, therefore, has no power over the Reality which waits silently at your core for full recognition. However, the persona will attempt to uphold the illusion which has trapped you all your life. The fortitude to calmly watch the persona's efforts without being moved is the guarantee that you will see the unreality of your persona shrivel in subjugation to the Reality of your Divine Presence.

Forgiveness works to repair the wounds inflicted on you by others, by circumstances or even by yourself. As discussed earlier in chapter two of this book, forgiveness can perform miracles in our lives if we can only give it licence to work through, and with, us. Love is the power source, the enabler of forgiveness. We have all met people who are unable to forgive because they are so much in the grip of hate. Hatred will not allow forgiveness and, thus, keeps you stuck in the mire of bitterness, resentment and pain. Where love is alive, forgiveness can flow freely and wash such negativity away like a healing stream. The clarity that forgiveness fosters, in turn, creates fertile ground for further fruits of Love's presence in our life to grow.

Where Love is present, you will also find kindness taking action to bring light and joy into our lives. There are times when an act of kindness would appear to be the most precious thing you could ever give or receive. People at the very limit of despair have been saved by a simple act of kindness, sometimes from a complete stranger. The heart that is the abode of love will meet the world with warmth, gentleness and consideration. The competitive, fear-driven persona can often be heard berating kindness as a foolish trait to be taken as a sign of weakness. Such souls as exhibit this trait can only expect to be exploited by the warrior class in the persona's rat race.

By such reasoning does the persona deny itself the sparkling riches hidden in our relationships where love is given reign to act. Genuine kindness (free of hidden motives) is amongst the most beautiful things we could encounter on our way here. To see kindness genuinely appreciated is also a thing of beauty. Love is our Friend and treats us with kindness, so much kindness. but the persona cannot perceive the warmth and kindness encompassing it in each moment. It seems to lack the means to discern the Love that sustains us all. However, when the persona reaches breaking point, it is often kindness that will take the rogue's hand and lead her/him into the presence of the Self. Kindness has this mysterious power.

Divine Love also brings us an indescribable order of happiness, joy, and bliss that is totally independent of all conditions. This immeasurable joy is intrinsic to your being and it is the state of union with the source of your being that reveals this bliss. This state of complete satisfaction is the limitless ecstasy residing as your innermost reality. In action here, this joy lifts you above the injuries and wounds being served up by the persona-constructed worldview. The inward dwelling joy acts to make you invincible in the face of the world drama. Its effect on you and those around you defies evaluation but it is enough to say that this bliss serves as a portal (for those touched by it) to timelessness and revelation. The sometimes-overwhelming nature of this bliss has to be balanced with a powerful sense of groundedness so that you can remain lucid and do your part here on earth. You can learn to keep this sublime state an unspoken secret, but, in many subtle ways, it will throw its light all around you.

The boundless source hidden in your seemingly limited form is the root of creativity, so your discovery of the truth about yourself and your experience of the vivifying force we speak of here, will release the creativity which is only natural to you. Our mistaken persona-inspired self-image has created a world where true creativity has been sacrificed to conformity and countless shades of expedience. Becoming your Self opens the door to a flow of creativity that comes into the world without stress or strain. This creativity arrives with a mysterious organising force that arranges synchronicities that would defy the persona's capacity to analyse them. Such creativity is merely an expression of your true nature which is, indeed, all-pervasive and, therefore, very much able to arrange chains of events of mind-boggling complexity.

This is, of course, happening all the time but when you awaken to your Divine source, these events begin to consistently accumulate as the working of Grace to bring you wonderful blessings. Have no doubt that this inspired creativity brings benefits to the whole creation aside from the beauty ushered into your own experience by its flow. This creativity may show up in how you relate to others, how you adorn your environment, how you cook your food, and how you live your daily life. It is not the sole property of artists, musicians and writers; this creativity borne of Love pours into every corner of every life surrendered to Love. It is the flower of life's exuberance.

Gratitude is one of the most wondrous facets in Love's vocabulary of action here amongst us. It is a channel for love's power to move through our lives as suggested earlier in the chapter entitled The Grateful Heart. To constantly feel gratefulness for your life and your numberless blessings is to become a Love power-station, a picture of love's radiant splendour here on earth. My friends, the lovers of Love, were such radiant souls and they were, indeed, constant in their gratefulness for life and for Love.

The proof of Love in action here amongst us is the growth of unity and the harmony which accompanies it. The persona's genius appears to lie in division and conflict. Its bond with fear, selfishness and greed sets it in opposition to any expansive sense of unity or harmony. For the persona, life is a fierce competition to be engaged with weapons blazing. At times, the warfare can appear to be overwhelming and the persona can retreat into self-pity, depression and despair. The appearance of genuine unity elevates those in its vicinity and creates beauty of the kind (described earlier in this chapter) found amongst the lovers of Love. This unity and harmony are the hope of humanity, but you can be certain that the persona will not achieve this wonderful estate, only the surrender to the Divine Presence within will deliver us to this paradise.

Free from the fetters arranged about the human soul by the egoic mind, we can experience the depths of unity and the exquisite joy of the harmony that is natural to the Self. Life is no longer a battlefield; it is now a festival to be savoured, full of grace and beauty. Here, all the fruits of Love in action on earth create heaven where there was once hell, joy where there was once only sorrow, peace where there was once only perpetual conflict.

This must happen for us individually. It must happen for us collectively, lest we seal our own self-destruction as a species living on planet Earth. We have the power to choose. Let us choose Love, as the alternative becomes more gruesome with each passing day. No matter which route humanity takes on the collective scale, nothing can separate you from the bliss that you are, nothing can separate you from Love. Whatever happens at the level of this dream of life on earth, know that, in the most profound sense possible, Love is all there is. The Unity which we are, is, in reality, Absolute.

Where does all the action take place? Always in the present moment. The direct experience of being can only ever take place in the here and now. To delve into existence, into the mystery of being, you must delve into the here and now. Only by living in the present moment can Love be expressed through you. The persona consistently inhabits the past and the future mentally, causing you to vacate the present moment. Again, the awareness of being only ever takes place in the here and now, so, this is the only place to meet the Self, to be and express Love; all the magnificent action takes place right here in the present.

By looking at ways in which Love acts through us, we can see clearly that it is a living force shaping our reality in discernible (as well as in mysterious) ways. When I think of people who embody Love in action, I can find no better example of this ideal than Harriet Tubman, a woman of legendary courage, commitment, compassion, patience, intuitive intelligence and devotion to the Divine principle. She was willing to make the ultimate sacrifice in the cause of freedom and human dignity. She was proof, if ever proof was needed, that Love acts through us to nurture the evolution of human consciousness. Harriet Tubman achieved seemingly impossible things due to her powerful connection to both the practical and the wholly mysterious facets of the movement which is Love in action here on earth.

Despite being born into slavery, Harriet came to discern her own connection to the indwelling Divinity. As a result, she became a most extraordinary and inspiring expression of our amazing potential to rise above adversity and limitation to discover our greatness. Her remarkable accomplishments stand out in the accounts of the tumultuous struggle against human bondage and oppression in this contemporary age. I hold her memory in the highest esteem, above all, because she surrendered herself to the higher Self and leaned so completely on that Self for guidance and protection in the midst of relentless peril. Love was paramount; this Supreme principle was her strength and glory.

Victory is certain

The essence of all our problems here is tied to the ignorance of our true identity. Until we rise above the state of ignorance, we have no hope of true satisfaction. All our challenges are really challenging us to wake up to the One that we truly are. Ironically, the more brilliantly clever and seemingly powerful the persona becomes in the world, the louder becomes the call for us to rediscover the Self. This is happening simultaneously on both the individual and collective planes. If you look at the nature of the problems that have plagued you throughout your life, no doubt you can identify patterns that appear to recycle and re-emerge consistently. These issues, these challenges are those best suited to breaking open the shell of ignorance in which we are cocooned. Your life has this in-built mechanism designed to shake you out of the coma of believing in duality and the seeming veracity of your persona. If we can appreciate this mystery at the centre of our mundane experiences here, we can realise we have cause to be grateful even for our challenges, if we can only begin to heed the call they represent.

Those pushed towards the abyss of despair by the challenges in their lives are often unwittingly closest to freedom. Our overwhelming problems can act to break the persona's domination over our attention. In the moment when all confidence in the persona's ability to bring the peace and enduring satisfaction we long for has perished, the opportunity arises for your heart to hear the silence that reveals the truth. Often, we must first tire of the ceaseless noise made by the persona, both in our own minds and in the world at large, before we can remember this sacred silence. So, bless your problems, bless the noise of your life, as they are seeking to reintroduce you to your Self. Surreptitiously pointing you towards Love, life is doing all it can to show us the inadequacy of fear to reveal the true glory of life to us. Everything, even the things that try us severely, presents us with the opportunity to rediscover the precious truth. Each problem is, therefore, not at all what it seems to be, just as you are not at all who you appear to be.

Right here and now, take a few moments to look deeply at the most challenging issue facing you in your life now. Ask Divine Intelligence to reveal to you what this challenge is calling forth in you. Be aware that when you ask for guidance in this manner, you may receive your answer in such a variety of ways that it is best to take the stance that life itself is communicating with you. You may receive a direct, immediate impression, you may get your answer in a dream, a portion of text may jump out at you from a book or an article, or you may see your answer in a film or hear it in a song. A stranger may tell you what you need to hear in passing, or a child may announce the answer to your conundrum. However the answer is presented to you, it will relate in some fundamental way to your need to rediscover your true identity. Any profound exploration of our life will draw us toward our Source. Even though this process is often imperceptible, the answer to our plight is forever available just beyond the veil created by the trance embodied by the persona.

Having accepted that every problem we face in our lives is, in fact, the same problem, the way opens for us to excavate the root of our basic dilemma. As a persona, we create a world of problems and experience a host of yet more problems we perceive as having been created by others. Turning toward the dimension of our being I have referred to as The Witnessing Presence, Awareness, Divine Intelligence, The Self, or Love, we can discern for ourselves that this eternal and pristine dimension of our being has no problems.

Observe the news on any media station on any given day and the reports of the unfolding narrative will reflect the fruits of the persona's labour; fear, intrigue, violence, deceit, exploitation, hatred and injustice are laid out before us to further feed the fear and anxiety that fuel the persona's quest for security. To turn your back on the persona and the drama it has created and to turn towards your Source is to escape the hold this illusion of duality has exerted on you all your life. Knowing that duality is a fleeting, changeful reality and that Supreme Love is the eternal, unchanging Reality, brings you into remembrance of who you really are, and this is the ultimate victory.

Instead of living your life from a place of fear and uncertainty, you live your life from a place of complete assurance that Grace supports and sustains you in the midst of all that the world has to display. The faculties of your spirit respond to the state of remembrance like flowers in a well-tended garden. The true power of your faculties and how they combine to express the Divine nature here on earth, become evident under the influence of the unity you have rediscovered in your own heart. These faculties provide the means to address the gross imbalances already produced by the persona. Healing, rejuvenation, justice, harmony, compassion and genuine prosperity can begin to flow into the world with each soul thus liberated by the surrender to Love.

At work in the phenomenal world, the ways of this Infinite Intelligence are complete. Love will give you the courage to fight fearlessly for justice, just as it will provide you with the wisdom and compassion to help another in their hour of need. It is the greatest warrior, just as it is the greatest peace-maker; it flows through every situation, finding expression in everything. Even when it could not seem at all possible, Love is present. Only when we have discovered this incomparable energy pulsing in every cell of our own being do we begin to be conscious of its Presence everywhere.

The Unity that is Love is not recognised by the persona. The persona exists in a state of ignorance regarding the essential unity underlying our existence. It is ignorant even of the essential unity sustaining each individual being. The persona ignores and violates the unity between our body, mind and soul, creating so much pain and suffering by doing so. The persona ignores and violates the unity between the various faculties of our being, creating so much dysfunction and limitation by doing so. Love is the unifying force that can heal the results of the persona's ignorance and violations. It will ease the process of awakening, and your re-establishment in your true, timeless, boundless and immaculate nature.

All the faculties of your being will be mobilised to give expression to your Divine nature here in the phenomenal world. Crucially, your subconscious mind will be cleansed of the negative and limiting beliefs and impressions which have been undermining your good. This can all happen purely on the basis of your sincere and profound surrender to Love. The true lover of Love throws off the cumbersome and often ugly robe of the persona to take on another raiment, which is the might of existence itself, beauty and power beyond words. The searing fire of the Truth has transcended the persona's ignorance and pride. Discovering this unity within yourself, you begin to see it everywhere and you are indeed humbled by the awe-inspiring realisation growing in your every moment.

Words cannot do justice to the glory which lies hidden in the fabric of our experience; this drawing breath, this being aware, presents us with riches that defy measurement, and yet, imprisoned in the perspective of the persona, life can appear to be a truly despairing encounter. I am here to say that the Truth does elevate you above everything that could harm you here. When my life seemed to be nothing more than a disaster that had led me to death's door, Grace introduced me to the amazing truth in saving my life and restoring my broken body. In time, I came to discover what exists at the various levels of my own being. The power that comes from bringing all these levels of being and their associated faculties into harmony and balance also revealed itself. The astonishing parallels between the architecture of my own being and that of the universe itself also came into view. In time, I came to understand that the whole universe stands on truth, harmony, balance, order and justice, just as my individual being exists on the basis of these same universal principles. When these principles are violated, degradation, decadence and suffering ensue. To claim the beauty, the peace, the joy, the redemption which is our birthright, we must have the courage to face the truth about how we have chosen to live. Nothing short of brutal honesty will do. Only the truth will open the door to our liberation.

It was vital for me to understand how I had violated the law that sustains us, to a degree that almost consigned me to an early grave. And this seeking the truth is a perpetual process; we must face the truth about the beliefs we hold in our subconscious mind that continue to limit or undermine us. We must face the truth regarding each situation that faces us and relate that truth to the law on which the universe stands. For example, if you find yourself in an abusive relationship, you must seek the truth about the nature of the abuse and why it is happening. You must seek the truth about what beliefs you hold in your subconscious mind about yourself and about relationships, that could help to create such a reality in your life. How is your experience violating harmony, balance, truth and justice? The truth you find by means of your brutally honest enquiry will set you free.

Having looked fearlessly at what is causing you harm, you are free to choose what you desire to replace that harm with. Now, see and feel the beauty and joy you desire instead of harm, and do this intensely and perpetually. Having faced the truth, take your attention away from what is causing you pain and give it powerfully to the consciousness of that which you truly desire that would adhere to harmony, balance, peace, order, truth and justice. Above all, delve into the fathomless depths of the truth regarding your true Divine identity. This is the deepest root of every problem in your life. This is the true theme of your life. You are not just your persona with its negative thoughts and feelings, you are the Self that is free of all such things. If all of these things are who you really are, you would not be able to drop them as you do in meditation or deep contemplation. Relieve your mind, allow fear to drop away, relax and these things are gone, leaving you in a state of peace, which is your true nature. When you abandon the baggage carried so faithfully and ardently by the persona and abide in the stillness, silence and peace that waits beyond the messy shroud of the person, you will, in that fathomless peace, discern the Self and you will discern its immutable, boundless nature which is inseparable from you. When this body has been reduced to dust, you will still, and forevermore, be this Divine Presence.

Every remarkable assertion in this book regarding your Divine identity can only be proven by virtue of your own direct experience. If you are sincere and courageous enough to defy the vice-like grip your persona has on your consciousness, you will discover the glory of the Truth about your Self for yourself. There are many paths to this Truth, but I would endorse, above all, the cultivation of 'the grateful heart' and being in love with Love as powerful means to speeding you home towards the realisation of the astounding Truth.

The search for spiritual fulfilment is often seen as an arduous path towards the attainment of virtues worthy of the spiritual seeker. Having arrived at a place of complete confidence regarding the truth of our essentially Divine nature, I can say that our task is not to attain any attributes or develop ourselves in any way apart from taking care to get our persona out of the way. We are already perfect and whole; it is just that our true nature is so much obscured by the conditioned self. It took such suffering for me to wake up to this reality, but this realization need not arrive via torturous means. This being in love with Love is so effective at smoothing the path to your immersion in the glory of your own truly pristine being. Love will bring you home in the most effortless way.

When you become in love with the Self, you will perpetually, happily and eagerly seek the company of your beloved and you will happily leave the persona and its drama behind. Established in the eternal love affair with the Self, all else will arrive gracefully, and everything will unfold in you naturally and with transcendental power. All the practices suggested in this book exist to encourage this getting to know and being in love with the Self. You are, thus, in love with life in the deepest way possible. I say this with heart-felt sincerity having been so much at odds with my own life for so long, but having remembered this Love, I now hold life to be sacred and beautiful beyond words. There is not one soul walking this earth that is not sustained by this Love and who would not be able to know this glory if they could abandon the impostor known as the persona. By some miraculous means, I came to know this Truth. From humiliating, lonely and, sometimes, almost deadly places, this Truth rescued me and set me free. In the depths of my heart, I know that the promise of freedom exists for every soul earnestly seeking this Truth. The dross of your imprisonment in the dream of the world drama is thus transformed into the gold of unity with your true eternal and Divine nature, which is Peace, which is Love.

For further information, the author can be contacted at: numightmaati@outlook.com

www.ingramcontent.com/pod-product-compliance
Lightning Source LLC
Chambersburg PA
CBHW072159100526
44589CB00015B/2282